Dazzling

★★★★★★ STARS

A GALAXY OF BLOCK PATTERNS

Carleen Parlato
&
Victoria Stuart

American Quilter's Society

P. O. Box 3290 • Paducah, KY 42002-3290
www.AQSquilt.com

Located in Paducah, Kentucky, the American Quilter's Society (AQS) is dedicated to promoting the accomplishments of today's quilters. Through its publications and events, AQS strives to honor today's quiltmakers and their work and to inspire future creativity and innovation in quiltmaking.

EDITOR: JANE TOWNSWICK
TECHNICAL EDITOR: HELEN SQUIRE
GRAPHIC DESIGN: LYNDA SMITH
COVER DESIGN: MICHAEL BUCKINGHAM
PHOTOGRAPHY: CHARLES R. LYNCH

Library of Congress Cataloging-in-Publication Data
Parlato, Carleen.
    Dazzling stars : a galaxy of block patterns / by Carleen Parlato and
Victoria Stuart.
        p. cm.
      ISBN 1-57432-769-0
   1. Patchwork--Patterns. 2. Quilting--Patterns. 3. Star quilts. I.
Parlato, Carleen. II. Title.
      TT835 .S78 20012
        746.46'041--dc21

                        2001003621

Additional copies of this book may be ordered from the American Quilter's Society, PO Box 3290, Paducah, KY 42002-3290, or online at www.AQSquilt.com.

Dedication

"All I ask is a tall ship, and a star to steer her by."
—John Masefield, 1902

To the Monday Night Quilters, past and present:
Ann S., Ann M., Peggy, Roberta, Margaret,
Carol, Tori, Nancy, and Vita Marie,
for their encouragement and
support in my transition from
quilter to teacher to designer.

To my husband, Gerry,
my children, Elaine and Alex,
and my brother, Bill,
who show me unconditional
love and tolerate the inevitable
decline in homemaking activities
that occur with each new
and exciting adventure I undertake.

Special thanks goes to Victoria Stuart,
without whom this book would
never have been "born."

Special dedication:
We are proud to honor the victims, their families, and
all the heroes of September 11, 2001.

Carleen Demshok Parlato

Acknowledgments

Imagine walking into a room filled with 200 strangers . . . and feeling immediately welcome, as if you had just returned home after a long trip. That's how I felt when I attended my first meeting of the Ocean Waves quilt guild in Miami in 1988.

I am incredibly grateful to the women I have met through quilting, who have given me their unconditional friendship, generosity, humor, and support, not only through quilt-times but also through life-times, especially the Monday Night Quilters: Carol Combs, Nancy Dunlap, Roberta Granville, Vita Marie Lovett, Margaret Marshall, Ann Mitchell, Peggy Schemenauer, Ann Shuflin, and Carleen Demshok Parlato.

To the quilters and the teachers, past and present, at The Quilt Scene, especially Lucy Mansfield, Stephanie Poet Cohen, Judy Duerstock, Lynn Kern, Edith Matthews, Rusty Miller, Brian Partin, Julie Sheckman, Jo Walters, and Bernice Yenkelun—you are the unsung heroes. You find the energy, enthusiasm, and creativity to design a hundred quilts a day for other people . . . and then go home and make even more. Every time I come to the store, I leave with a greater appreciation for your exceptional talents and your willingness to share them with others. Thank you for helping me learn the techniques and skills I needed to grow as a quilter and for giving me the confidence to teach what I love the most.

To my Mom, Joan, thank you for everything. You are the center of my universe.

And Carleen– since the day you taught me my first quilting stitches, you opened a door to a new world of creativity and discovery that continues to bring new wonders every day. It has been one of the greatest pleasures of my life to come up with the words to describe the designs you spent ten years of your life creating. I am thrilled to see your "dream stars" come to life, and I am so glad that your "inspired obsession" turned out to be contagious.

Victoria Stuart

Table of Contents

Foreword

As a novice quilter, I fell in love with eight-pointed stars, such as the Lone Star and its many variations; however, my inexperience led to frustration as I tried to make eight points come together accurately in the middle of a block. Several years and many star blocks later, when I was drafting an eight-pointed star pattern of my own one day, I suddenly realized that I could sew nine rectangular units together to create an eight-pointed star block that would be as easy to piece as a nine-patch, yet have all the flair and design potential of the Lone Star pattern.

The 48 blocks I designed for this book are the result of ten years of my "inspired obsession" with stars, as I dreamed, graphed, designed, and experimented to create new variations of the basic star pattern. Star blocks offer a perfect framework for exploring new ways to use color and value to produce the effect of dimensionality, and they are also a great format for showcasing bold fabrics and stripes to create visual interest.

With all the time that has passed since I struggled to piece my first eight-pointed star, stars still remain a source of enjoyment and creative satisfaction to me. I hope that the blocks in this book will be the same for you.

Carleen Demshok Parlato

Introduction

Quilters of every age and every land have always loved stars. In America, they shine throughout our history: our flag is brimful with them, our national anthem glorifies them, our eyes are full of them. It's no wonder then that stars twinkle in so many American quilts, from simple Ohio Stars to more intricate designs, like Seven Sisters, Lone Stars, Broken Stars, Compass Roses, Sawtooth Stars, Feathered Stars, Variable Stars, Martha Washington's Stars, Spinning Stars, and a thousand other variations.

This book features 48 original star blocks designed by Carleen Demshok Parlato. All of the blocks are the same 12" finished size, and most contain corner, side, and center units that are interchangeable, which creates nearly unlimited potential for coming up with your own unique star blocks. You'll love how the unique center treatments of these designs enable you to create gorgeous eight-pointed star blocks without the frustration of trying to match all eight seams in the center.

The templates on pages 35–48 are designed to ensure easy and precise piecing every time. You can trace them onto template material, or purchase a customized set of acrylic templates to use with a rotary cutter (see "Resources," on page 110).

As you browse through the dazzling star blocks on pages 18–33, you'll notice small thimbles next to each one, showing the level of sewing skill required for making that design. For example, a block with one thimble indicates a design that is easy enough for a beginner, while blocks with two or three thimbles show patterns that require a bit more piecing skill. If you're a beginner, start out by making a few of the easier blocks, and you'll soon be ready to explore the entire galaxy of designs.

We hope you will think of this book as your pathway to the stars, and let the gallery of quilts on pages 59–95 inspire you to fill your universe with dazzling star quilts of your own.

Happy stargazing!

Carleen Demshok Parlato and Victoria Stuart

Great Points about Dazzling Stars

Dazzling Star blocks feature basic rectangular sections pieced together like a nine-patch block. There are designs easy enough for beginners, as well as more challenging patterns for experienced quilters. Here are a few other features.

Nubbed-to-Fit Templates

Dazzling Stars are a dream to sew, because the templates are engineered to fit together precisely. They are "nubbed-to-fit," which means that the corners of triangular points on each template are precision-trimmed, so that each template will match up exactly with adjacent patches. This means that you will not need to do any trimming after you stitch the seams of units together. If you're a beginner, you'll find that templates like these make your piecing much easier and more enjoyable. If you are a more experienced quilter, you'll appreciate both their precision and the timesaving aspect of not having to trim the points on triangles.

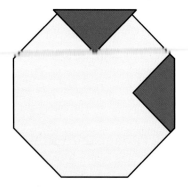

Large Center Spaces

The centers of the star blocks in this book are large squares or octagons, so you won't have to worry about matching eight seams at the centers of your blocks.

The large center spaces also give you a wide open area for featuring some fabulous fabrics from your stash, or showcasing your favorite quilting designs.

Easy Unit Construction

Most of the blocks consist of nine pieced units that are sewn together the same way as a simple nine-patch block.

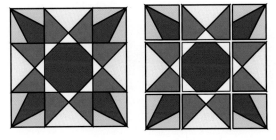

The shapes in a few of the blocks make it necessary to sew them together "in the round," which often gives you a chance to increase the effect of dimensionality in the star.

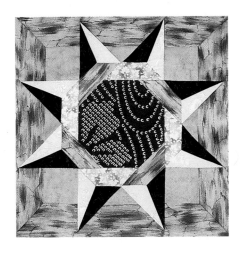

Mix-and-Match Shapes

You can vary the positions of units in the middle, side, or corner portions of a block to create your own variation of a star design, or combine units from different blocks into a design of your own.

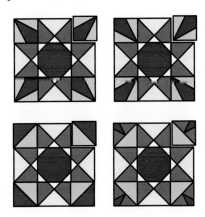

Secondary Designs

Many of the blocks form secondary (sometimes, even tertiary) designs when they are placed side by side. Block #10 is a good example of this; the other shaded block drawings provide more ideas. This versatility can give you even more design freedom when planning your quilt. You can set your stars on point, side-by-side, with or without sashing, or just use a single star for stunning effect!

Dimensionality

The three-dimensional quality of these block patterns can be enhanced by your placement of light and dark fabrics within the star shapes. Use the tips and guidelines on pages 13-16 to choose a dynamite color combination that will take your stars into the sixth dimension . . . and beyond

Lift Off!
Getting Started

You have a whole new universe of designs to explore! See which ones you would like to make. You can create interesting secondary designs when the corner units in each block come together in a quilt. Notice the way that light, medium, and dark shades are used in the diagram of each block, and keep these value placements in mind as you begin to think about a stellar combination of fabrics for your star blocks.

Start with a Focus Fabric

Dive into your stash or visit your local quilt shop to find one really sensational fabric you'd like to feature in the center area of your star block. As you search for the perfect focus fabric, look for colors you love, motifs that appeal to you, and let this focus fabric become your guide for choosing other coordinating fabrics.

If your choice of focus fabric is a colorful batik, a bright, bold jungle print, or a whimsical, romantic print like these, you can use related fabrics and colors for the star points that will enhance the overall effect you are trying to create in your block.

If you love pastels, let the lines of the star design rather than a high degree of color contrast provide the visual impact in your block.

For a more dramatic effect, start with a colorful, large-scale floral print and showcase individual flowers in the center squares of your blocks. Or go for a casual English garden look, by cutting large-scale focal prints randomly, rather than centering floral motifs within the center areas.

Vary the Values

As you select your fabrics, the main thing to remember about color is that dark and dull colors tend to recede, or fade into the background visually, while light and bright colors seem to "pop out," or come forward in a design. The dimensional aspect of your star blocks will vary greatly, depending on where you place your colors; when the *value* (lightness or darkness) is the same throughout a group of colors, the warm colors (reds, oranges, yellows) will appear dominant visually, and the cool colors (blues and greens) will seem to recede into the background.

In the first color scheme*, both the red and blue have the same value; notice how the red star points really seem to blaze, while the smaller blue areas are not as visually prominent.

In the next example**, a monochromatic color scheme is shown where the light and dark blues give the star an added feeling of dimension.

In this pastel palette***, soft, subtle colors are featured, which can still create enough contrast in value to give the star a dimensional quality.

*

**

***

Using Stripes

Dazzling Star blocks are the perfect stage for letting linear fabrics perform at their best. You can use stripes and plaids in any area of a block, but as shown in the following two designs, they become "star attractions" in the points of a star or as the frame around the outer edges of a block.

There are basically three types of linear designs: *true stripes*, *wavy* (unmatched) *stripes*, and *"generally" linear designs*.

True Stripes

As you can see in the photo below, true striped fabrics feature very straight lines that march in precise order. As a general rule when using fabrics like these, remember that the greater the level of contrast between the colors and the straighter the lines, the more care it will take to line them up correctly when you cut and sew together the pieces for a star block.

Wavy Stripes

Unmatched stripes give you all the joys of using linear fabric, without the stress! Since the lines are not spaced evenly, they do not need to matched precisely. In fact, these types of fabrics are usually more interesting and add more energy to a star design if they *don't* match exactly.

Generally Linear Designs

Fabrics like these, with less distinctive lines that still create a feeling of directional movement, fall into the category of "generally" linear designs. They will give your blocks the look of dimension while requiring no matching. Just remember to keep the grain lines going the same direction in each piece.

Galactic Visions
Creating Special Effects

The tips and ideas in this section will help you explore the potential for creating a variety of special effects and beautiful secondary designs in your quilt.

Visualize Your Universe

Once you've picked your star block and selected your fabrics, it's helpful to create a mock-up of one block to make sure that the fabric that looked so great on the bolt will look the way you want in your star. For example, if you are trying to emphasize the points of the star, do they stand out as you imagined or are they eclipsed by the background fabric? Does the striped fabric you picked work best in the corners or in the center square? Going through this process will help you visualize the finished star and make sure it's what you like.

Use the templates and cut enough pieces for your block and lay them out on a table in the configuration of the star. You don't have to sew anything. That way, if something doesn't look the way you want it to, you can change your plan.

Note: Viewing your blocks on a design wall is a great way to visualize your finished quilt. Use a piece of batting the size of your finished quilt and lay it on a table, tack it to a wall, or hang it over a door. When you place your fabric pieces on it, they will "stick" and allow you design freedom. If you are computer savvy, you can also scan the block patterns and your fabrics into your computer and use a quilt design program to achieve the same result.

Showcase Special Fabrics

Some special fabrics, such as lamé, silks, or woven plaids, can provide extra sparkle and dimension in a star quilt, so don't be afraid to try them in small amounts. To make lamé easier to handle, iron lightweight, fusible interfacing (non-woven) to the back of the fabric before you cut it. Remember, though, that quilts with lamé in them need to be dry-cleaned rather than laundered in a washing machine.

Kaleidoscope Effects

Dazzling Star blocks #19 through #29 on pages 24–27 are the best designs to choose for creating a kaleidoscopic look because they each have a center that is made up of four triangles joined together to form a square. Where these triangles come together, you can create the look of a wonderful kaleidoscope by using small border prints, stripes, or florals.

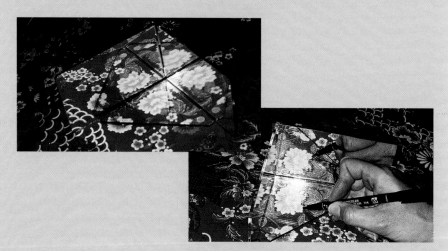

Step 1

Use a pair of hinged mirrors to identify a special motif in your fabric and see how it would look when reflected in kaleidoscopic fashion.

Step 2

Lay a clear plastic or acrylic template on top of the design and trace around the edges of the motif with a fine-tip permanent marker.

Step 3

When you cut the pieces for your block, center the outline on the template on top of the motif you want to capture. This will make all of your pieces exactly the same, producing a kaleidoscopic effect when the block is stitched together.

Step 4

The lines drawn on your template can be easily removed when you complete your project; simply moisten a small cotton wipe with rubbing alcohol, and swab the lines gently until they rub away.

Stars-within-Stars

The center portion of Dazzling Star block #30 creates a star-within-a-star effect. Use the light and dark shades in the block diagram on page 27 as a guide to choosing light and dark fabrics that will create the same effects in your blocks.

Secondary Designs

Also consider the design potential in the corner units; when blocks like these are set side-by-side, interesting shapes can emerge in the corners. When you page through the designs in the Galaxy of Dazzling Star blocks on pages 17–33, take a close look at the corner units in each block and try the following ideas for using them to create exciting secondary designs like the ones in these quilts.

When the corners of four blocks meet, think about featuring a different fabric in one corner triangle of each block. Here, a navy print forms a square-on-point at the center of the quilt.

Try eliminating some corner shapes. In this quilt, the long, red triangles create the look of a stylized pinwheel at the center of the quilt, while they are omitted at the outer corner of each block, only to appear again in units that complete the pinwheel shapes at the sides of the quilt.

Corner units with diagonal shapes can enhance a feeling of movement in a dramatic quilt design. What kind of design variation could you create if you rotated the corner units in the opposite direction?

Varying the fabric used within shapes in some corner units can produce beautiful special effects, like the kaleidoscopic motif at the center of the quilt on the previous page.

3-D Stars

To enhance the three-dimensional effect in your Dazzling Star block, use lighter, brighter fabrics for the star points (blocks that feature Template M) and deeper, darker fabrics for the corner, secondary star points (blocks that feature Templates B and E). The light and bright fabrics will seem to advance visually, while the darker fabrics will recede, giving your star greater depth and dimension.

Both of these stars are the same Dazzling Star block #43, but notice how different they look due to the difference in the placement of lights and darks. The stars seem to spin in different directions, too.

Other Techniques

Dazzling Star blocks with large center octagons provide a wide open field for including beautiful appliqué, silk-ribbon embroidery, pen-and-ink inscriptions, and photo transfers. Be creative — the sky's the limit!

Note: The ribbon embroidery design shown in this block is "Spring Bouquet" from *Ribbon Embroidery Alphabets* by Barbara Baatz. American School of Needlework, Inc.

Galaxy
of 48 Dazzling
Star Blocks

There are two diagrams for each Dazzling Star block.
One is a line drawing that shows the templates needed to make
the block, as well as the grain lines for each of the patches.

The second drawing of each block is a color illustration
to guide you as you select your own fabrics.

The little thimbles next to each design indicate
the skill level needed to make the block.

One thimble indicates a design that is super easy. *Two* thimbles
point to a block that is easy. *Three* thimbles signal designs
that feature more pieces or gentle, set-in seams
that require a bit more care and attention.

All of the blocks are the same 12" finished size, and most contain corner,
side, and center units that are interchangeable, which creates nearly
unlimited potential for coming up with your own unique star blocks.

Block 1

Block 2

Block 3

Dazzling Stars: A Galaxy of Block Patterns — Parlato & Stuart

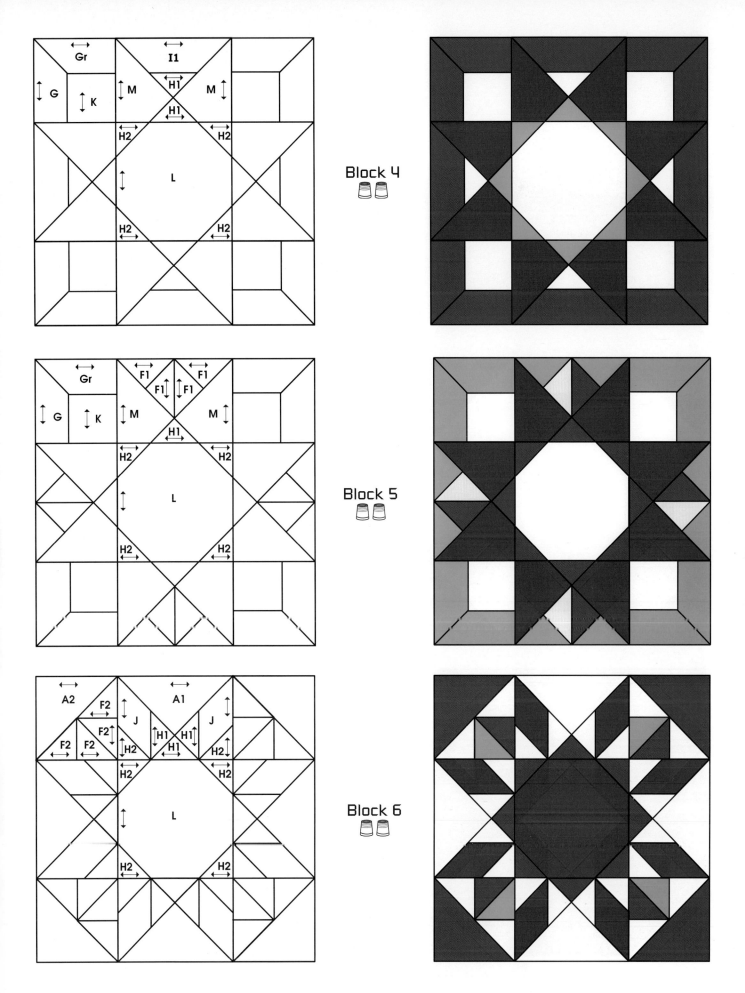

Block 4

Block 5

Block 6

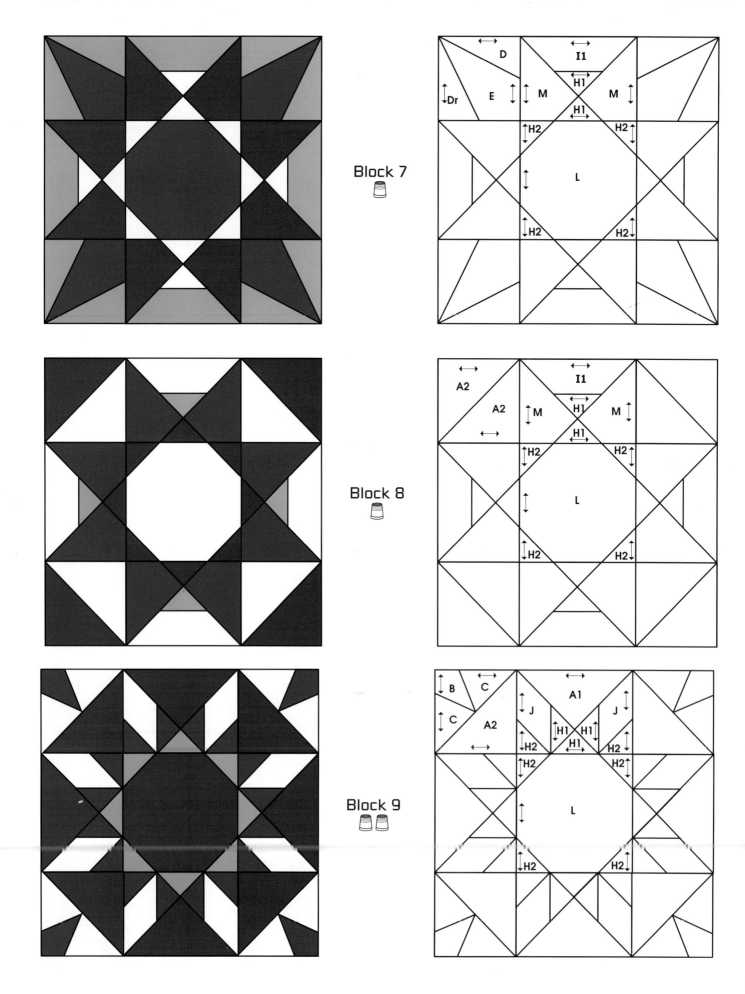

Block 7

Block 8

Block 9

Dazzling Stars: A Galaxy of Block Patterns — Parlato & Stuart

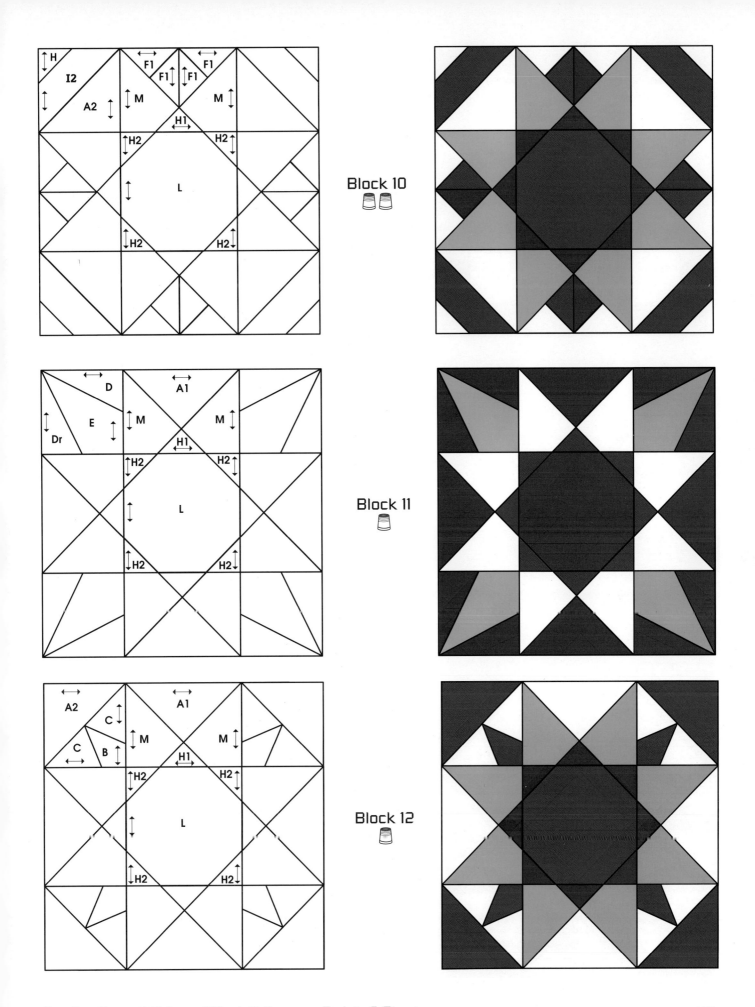

Block 10

Block 11

Block 12

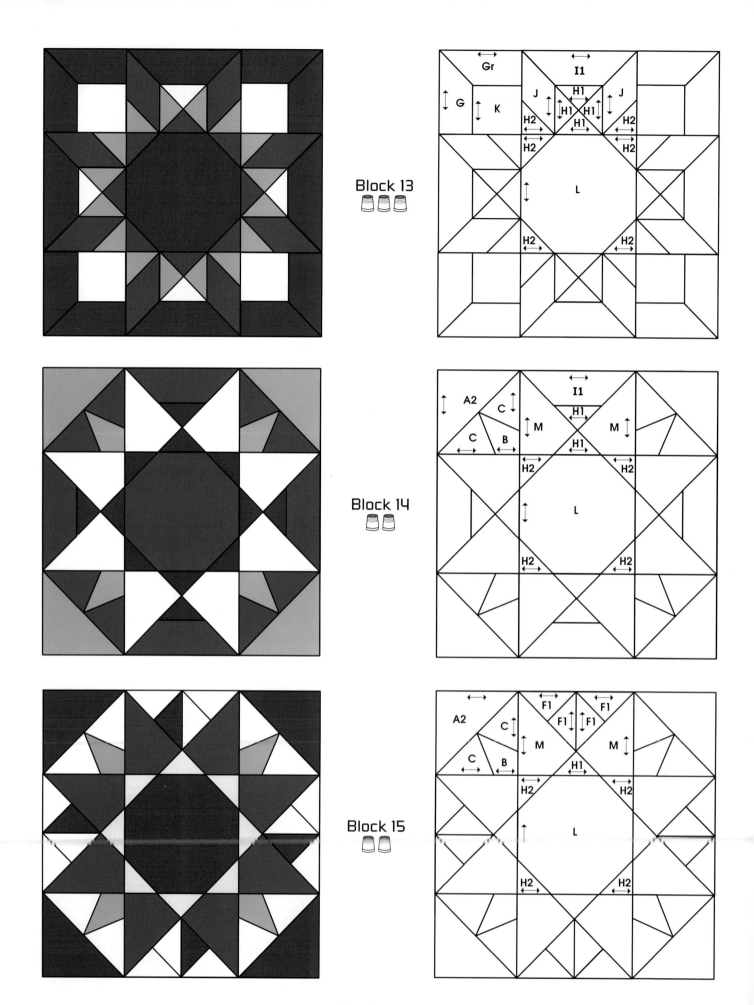

Block 13

Block 14

Block 15

Dazzling Stars: A Galaxy of Block Patterns – Parlato & Stuart

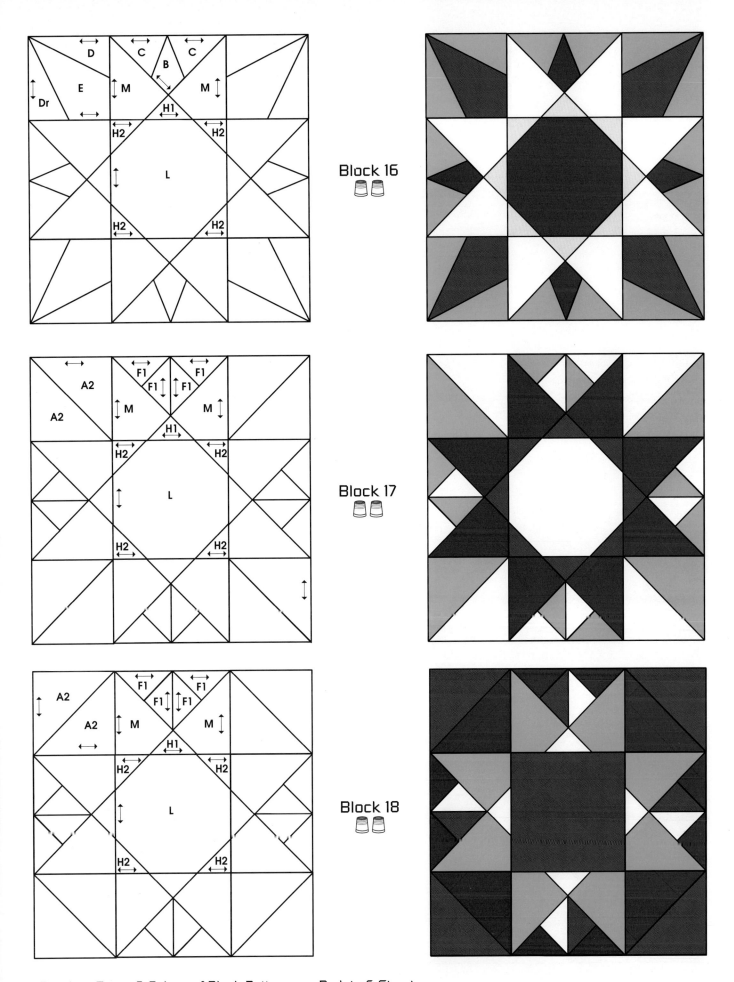

Block 16

Block 17

Block 18

Dazzling Stars: A Galaxy of Block Patterns — Parlato & Stuart

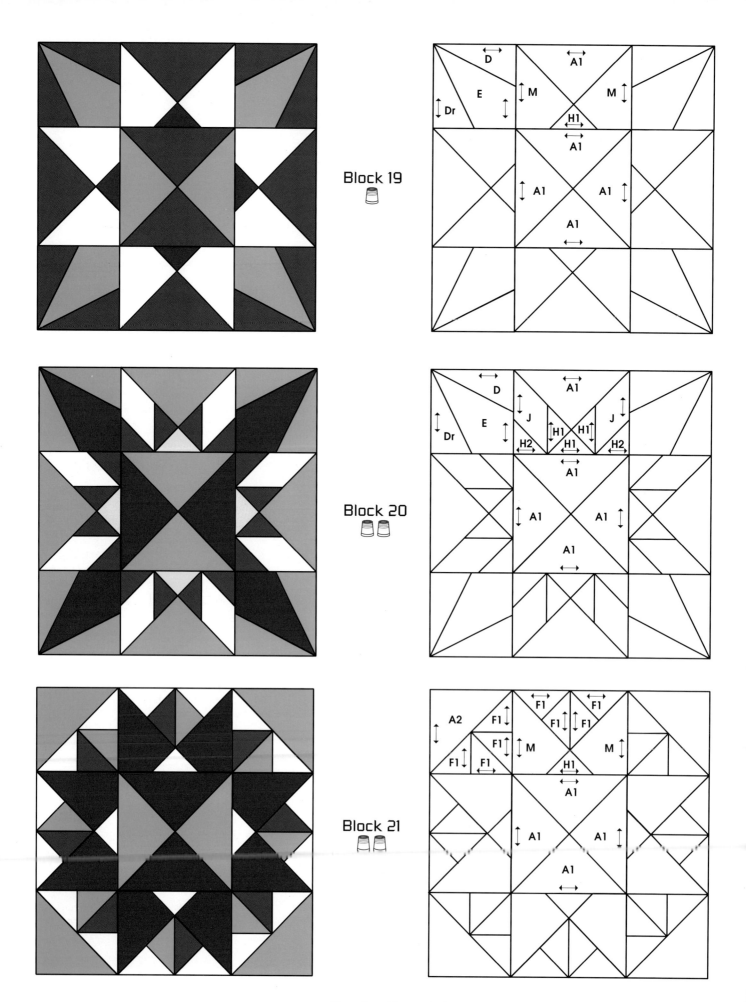

Block 19

Block 20

Block 21

Dazzling Stars: A Galaxy of Block Patterns – Parlato & Stuart

Block 22

Block 23

Block 24

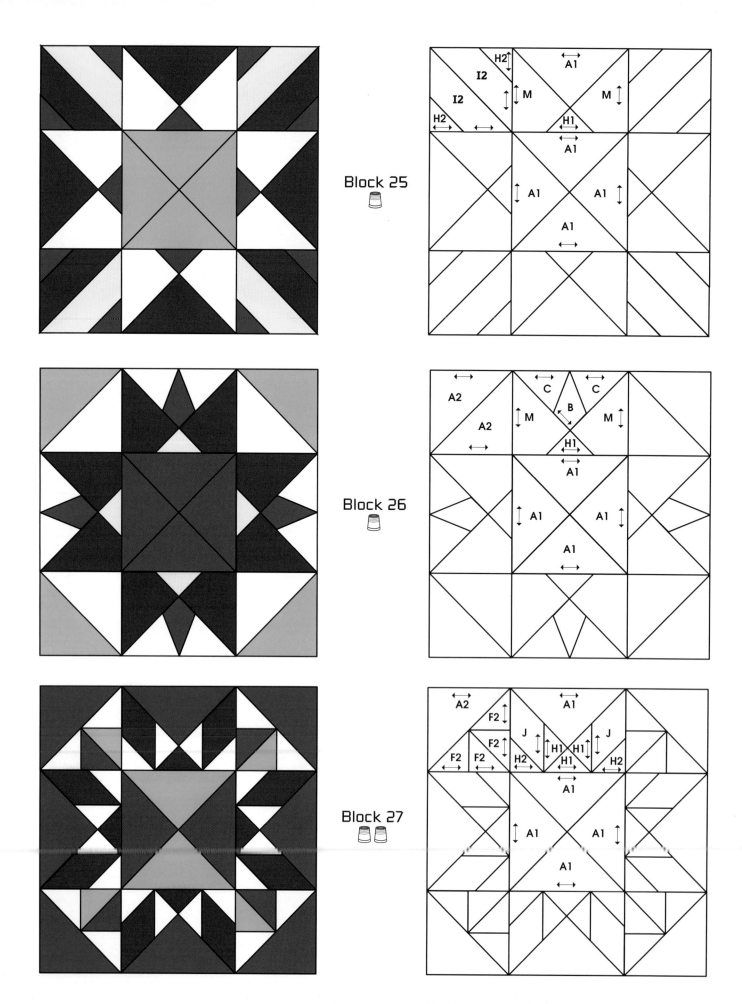

Block 25

Block 26

Block 27

Dazzling Stars: A Galaxy of Block Patterns — Parlato & Stuart

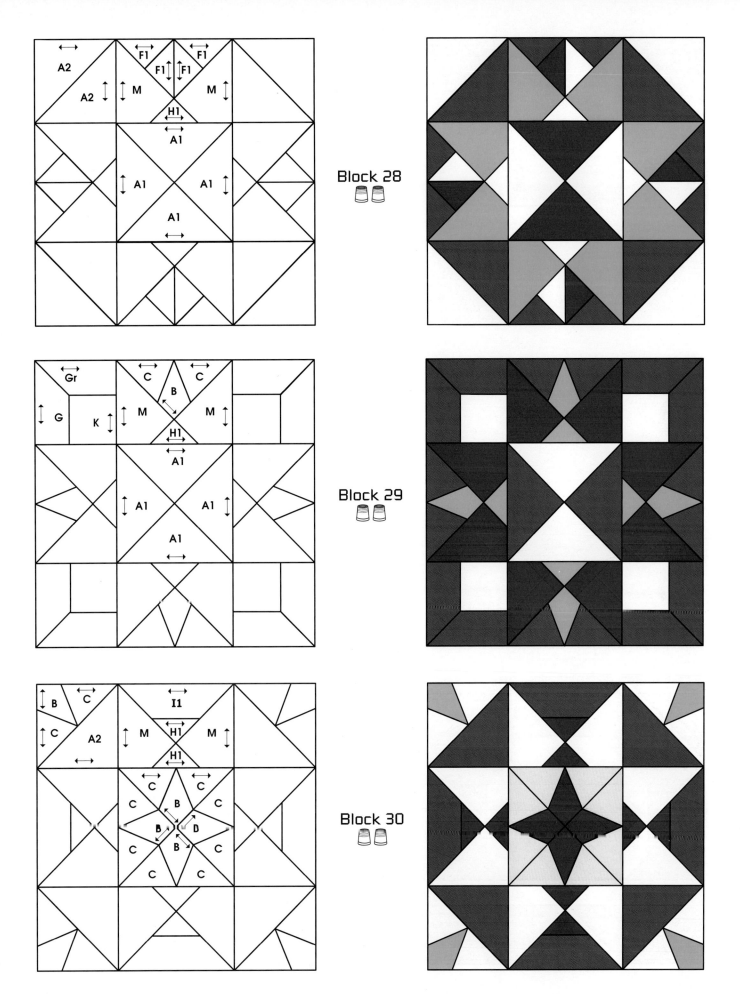

Block 28

Block 29

Block 30

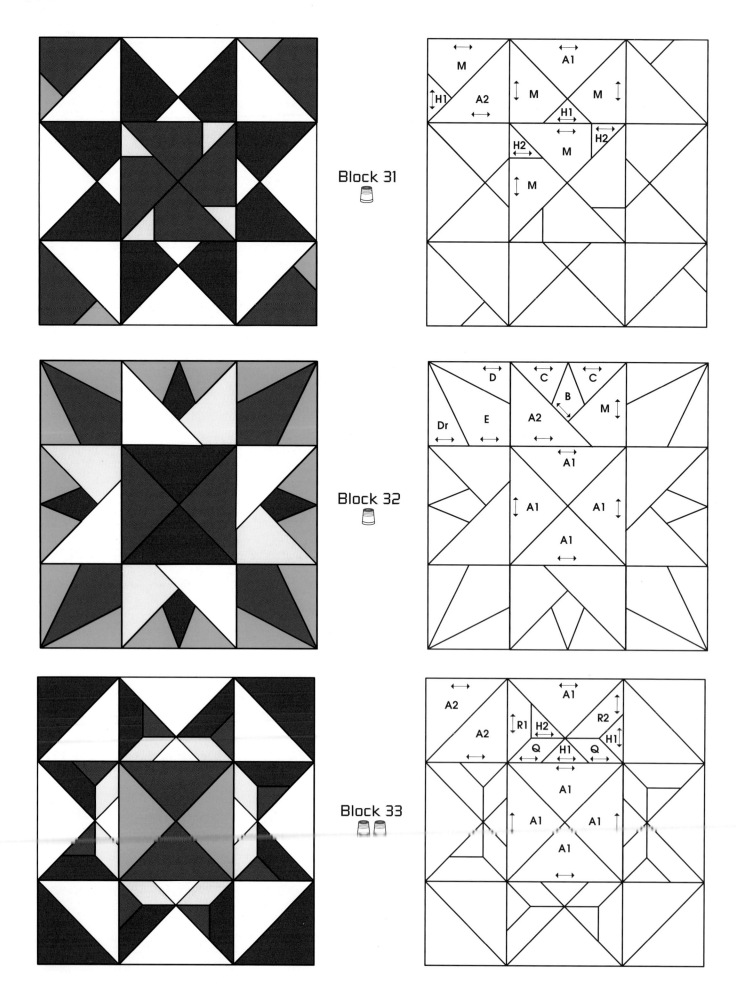

Block 31

Block 32

Block 33

Dazzling Stars: A Galaxy of Block Patterns — Parlato & Stuart

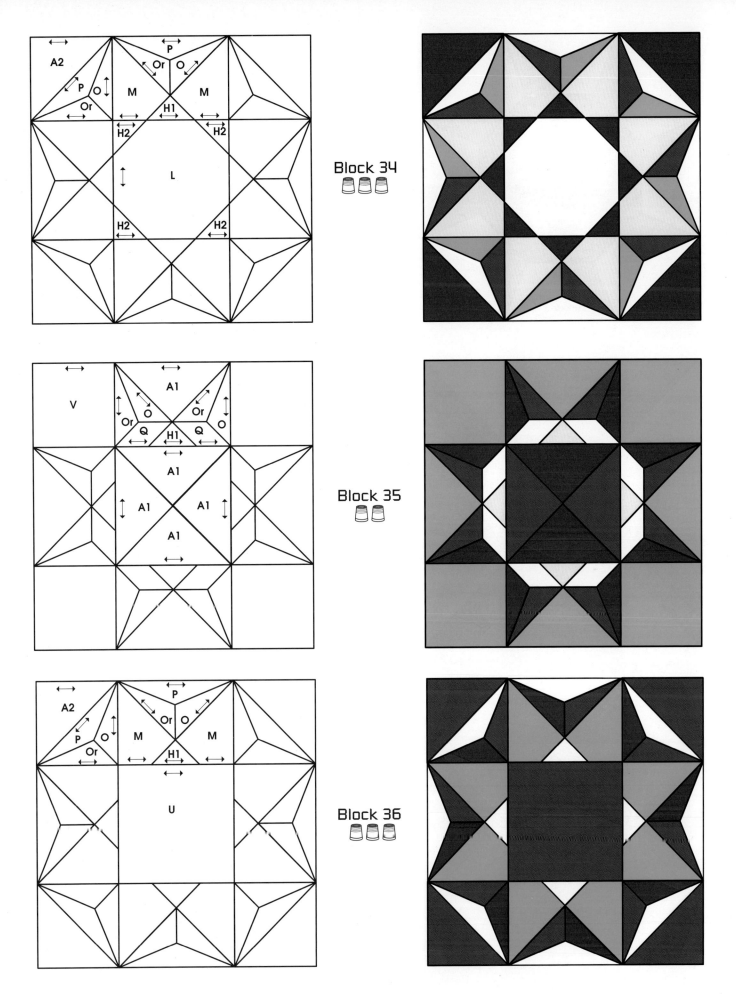

Block 34

Block 35

Block 36

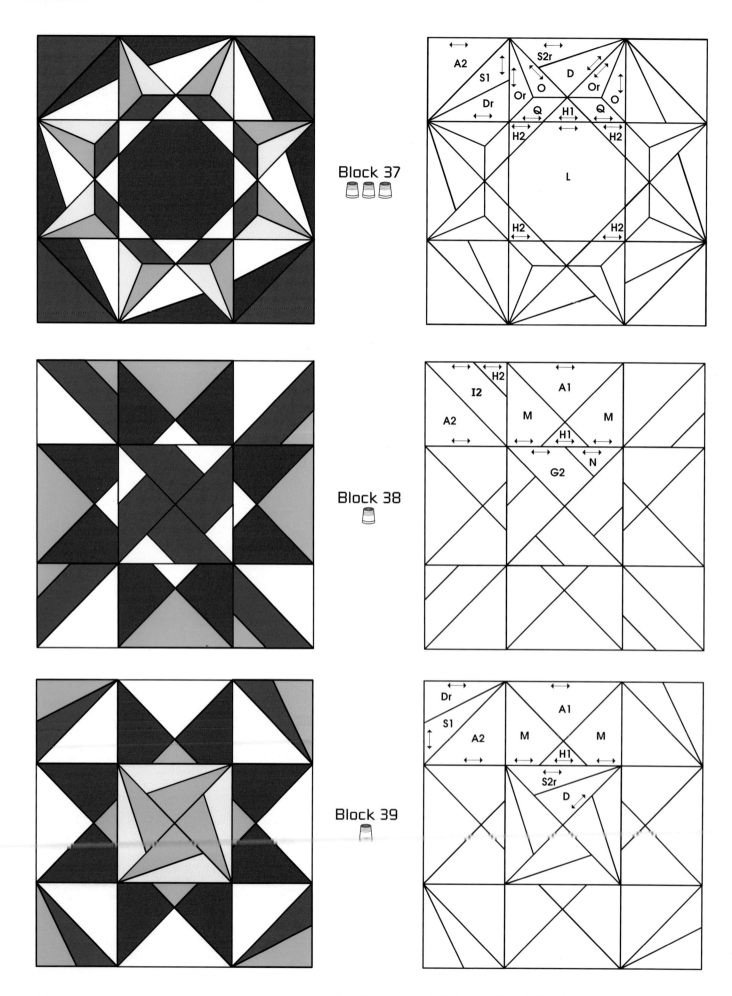

Block 37

Block 38

Block 39

A2 S1 S2r D
Dr Or O Or O
Q H1 Q
H2 H2
L
H2 H2

H2
I2 A1
A2 M M
H1
N
G2

Dr A1
S1
A2 M M
H1
S2r
D

Dazzling Stars: A Galaxy of Block Patterns — Parlato & Stuart

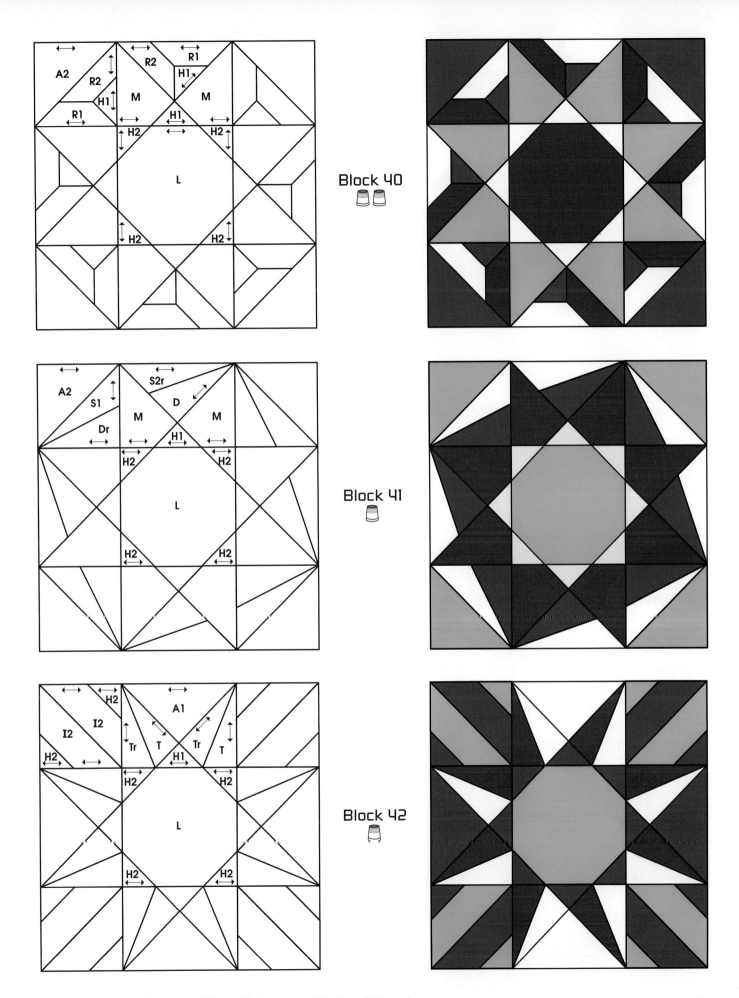

Block 40

Block 41

Block 42

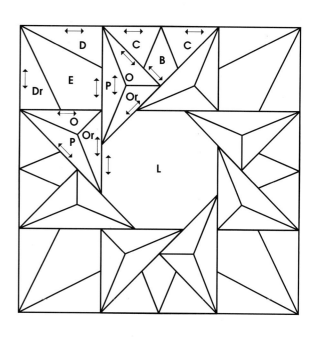

Block 43

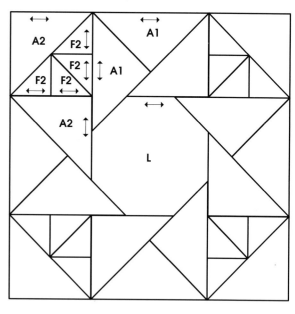

Block 44

Block 45

Dazzling Stars: A Galaxy of Block Patterns – Parlato & Stuart

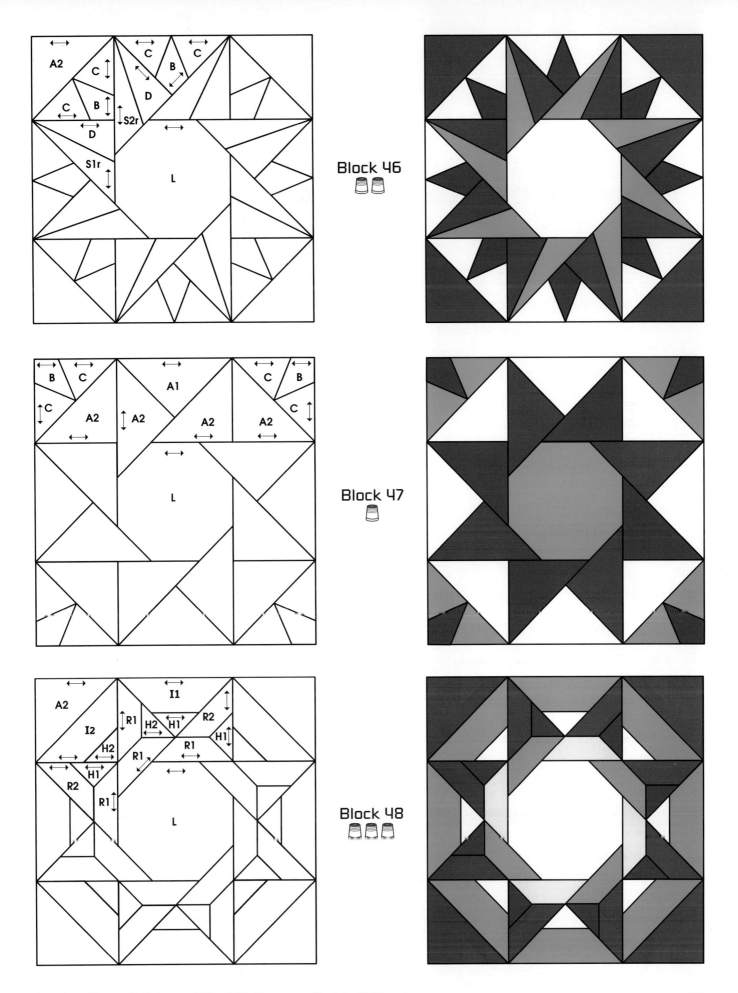

Block 46

Block 47

Block 48

Star Templates & Cutting Diagrams

Templates A through V are provided on the following pages.
You can either trace these shapes onto template plastic and cut them out
or purchase a set of acrylic templates designed for rotary cutting.

Preparation

Using a permanent marker, label the top side of each template with its letter, or attach a piece of masking tape to the template and write the letter on the tape. Underline each letter so that you will be able to tell the difference between H and I, or C and U if the templates get turned around.

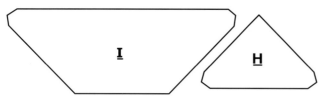

Tip: Placing sandpaper dots or squares on the reverse side of each template will help prevent the templates from sliding around on your fabric as you cut.

Grain-line Arrows

Some of the templates may be used in different positions in a star block, so different grain lines have been marked on each template, depending on their position in the block. These grain line arrows, and the Cutting Diagrams, shown with the templates, will help you cut your pieces correctly. For example, the H1 and H2 templates are cut with the straight-of-grain in different positions for stability.

Make sure to check the grain line arrows on the line drawing for each block, as well as the cutting guides. Place the templates on the straight-of-grain of your fabric,

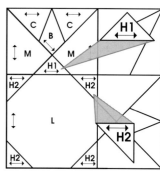

following the grainline arrows, and cut out the pieces for your star blocks.

However, there may be times when you intentionally decide to cut pieces off-grain, perhaps to take advantage of a special motif in your fabric or to position a linear design a certain way. In this photo, the short side of the first star point template is placed so that it will lie on the lengthwise grain of the fabric in the finished block. The second and third examples show the short side of the star point template placed deliberately off grain so that the stripe in the fabric is placed from the tip to the bottom or across the star point shape.

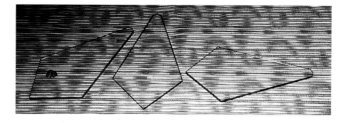

Templates and Cutting Diagrams
for Dazzling Star Blocks

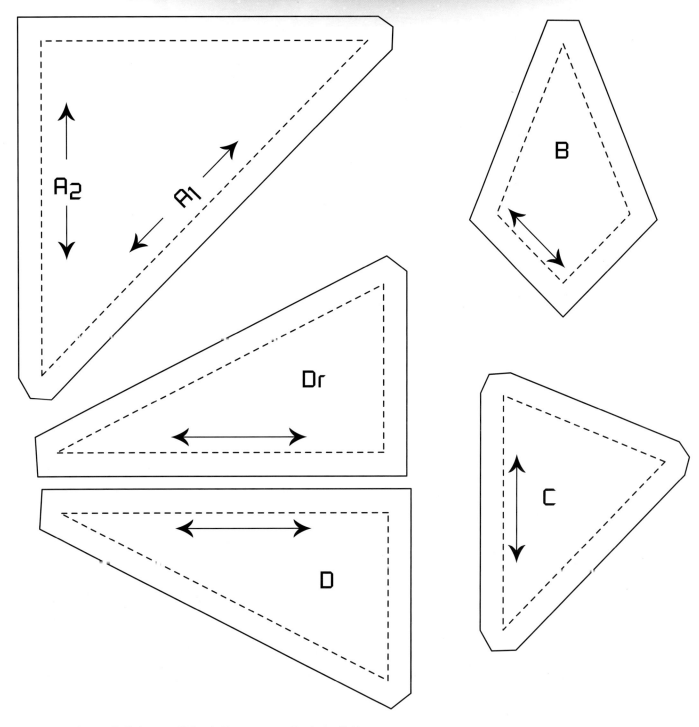

Cutting Guidelines

Use the following suggestions to help save time and make the best use of your fabric.

Fold your fabric in half lengthwise, matching the selvages. If you like to cut through four layers at once, fold it in half lengthwise again. To cut each set of pieces for your Dazzling Star block, start by cutting a strip across the width of your folded fabric, following the measurements listed under Cutting Diagrams; then position your templates on the fabric and cut them out according to the diagrams.

The (r) next to the large letter on a template indicates that you will need to cut a reverse image of that template. For example Dr indicates Template D reversed. You will get a reversed image automatically when your fabric strip is folded as indicated.

Sometimes you will need to cut *only* an asymmetrical shape *or* its reverse image (such as Template D, G, O, S, or T) for a block. For example, see the way Template D is used in Dazzling Star block #46. There may also be occasions when you *wish* to cut a template shape and its reverse image from two different fabrics. For example, see the way Templates O and Or are used in Dazzling Star block #35. In each of these cases, cut these shapes from a single layer of fabric.

Cutting Diagrams for Dazzling Star Templates

Cut your fabric strips in the widths listed for each template needed for the Dazzling Star block you want to make, and use the cutting diagrams to positioning the templates correctly on the strips.

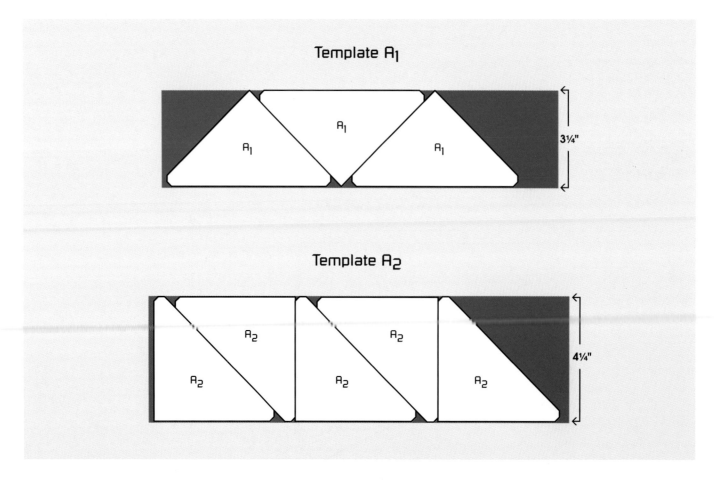

Template A₁

Template A₂

Template B

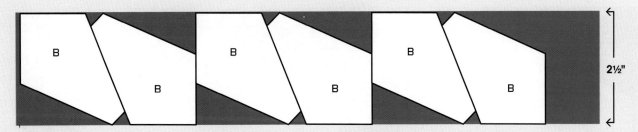

2½"

Template C

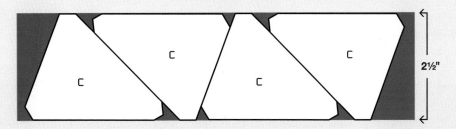

2½"

Template D

Cutting Template D from a folded
strip of fabric will give you an
equal number of D and Dr pieces.

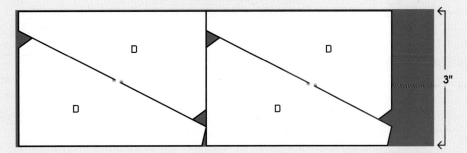

3"

Cutting Diagrams

Template E

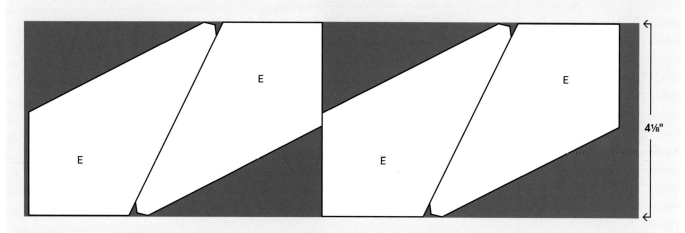

4⅛"

Template F₁

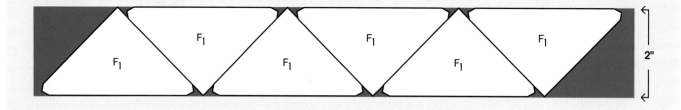

2"

Template F₂

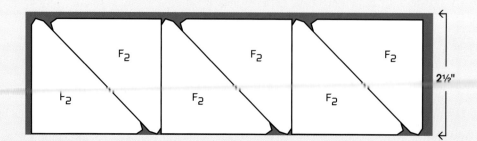

2½"

Template G₁

Cutting Template G₁ or G₂
from a folded strip of fabric will
give you an equal number of
G₁ and Gr₁ or G₂ and Gr₂ pieces.

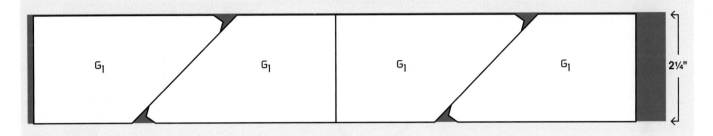

2¼"

Template G₂

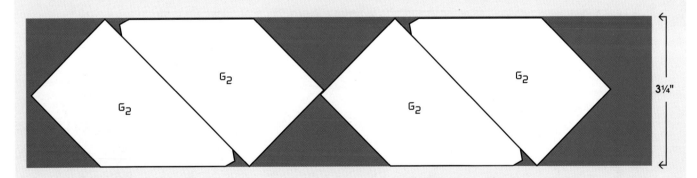

3¼"

Template H₁

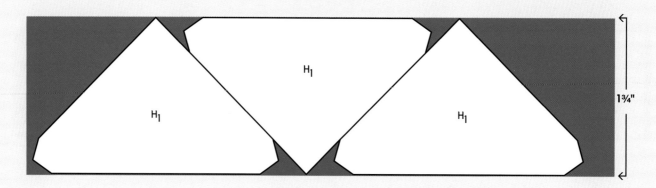

1¾"

Template H₂

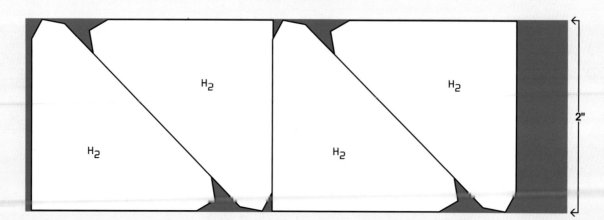

2"

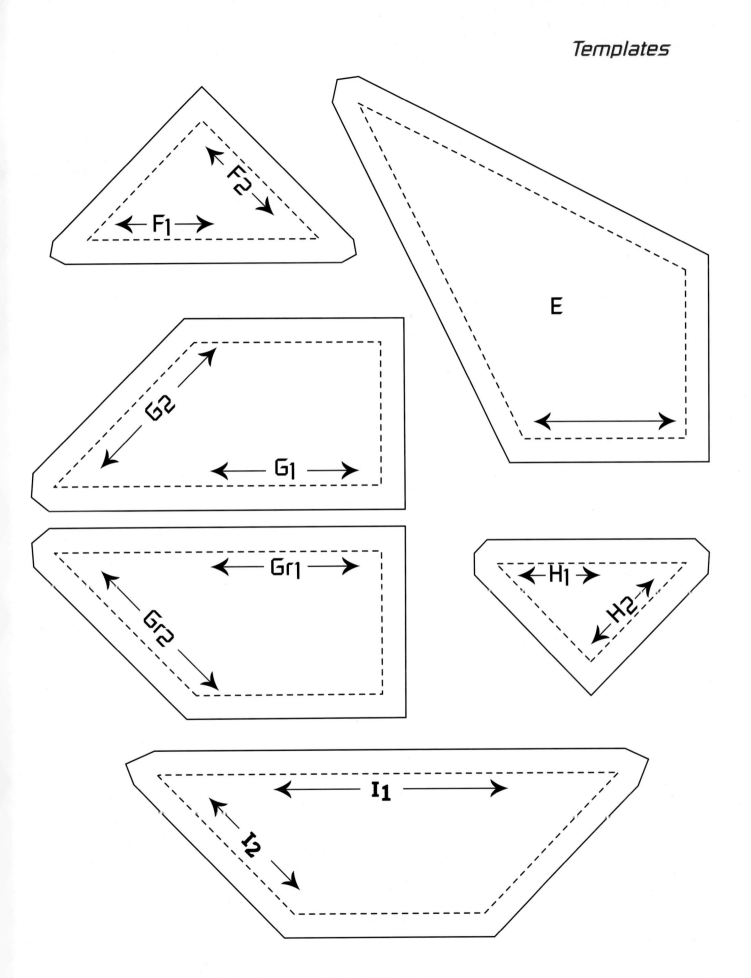

Cutting Diagrams

Template I₁

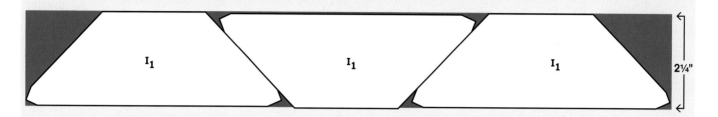

2¼"

Template I₂

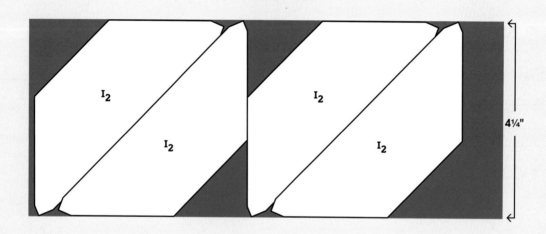

4¼"

Template J

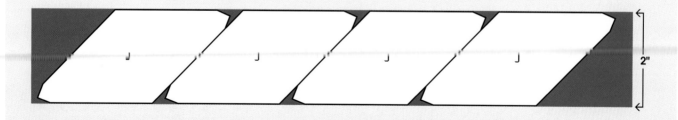

2"

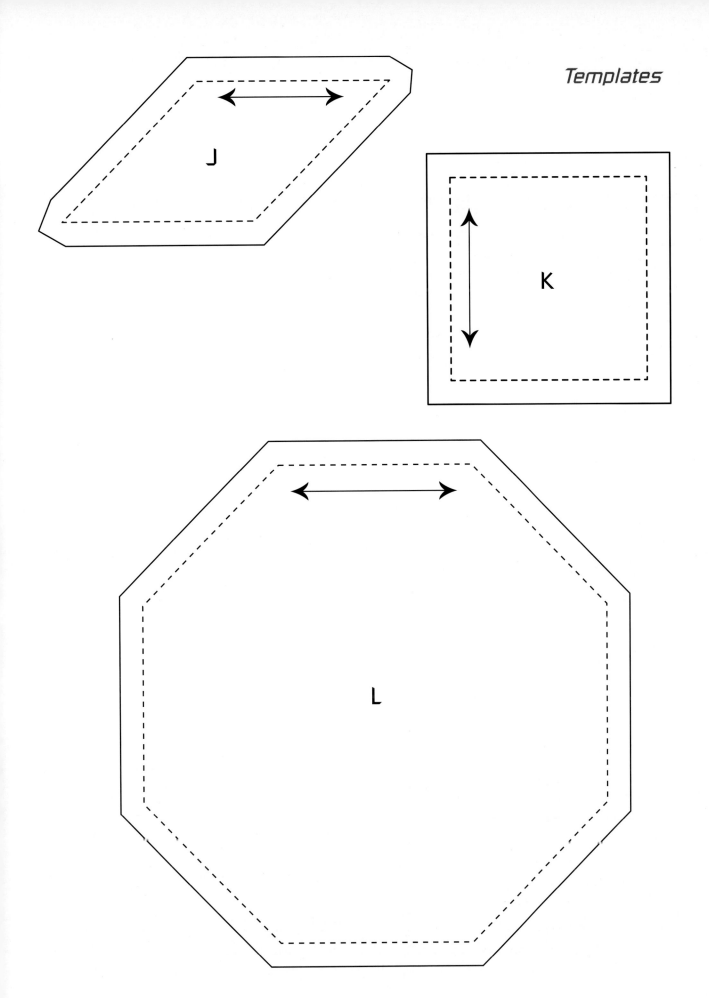

J

K

L

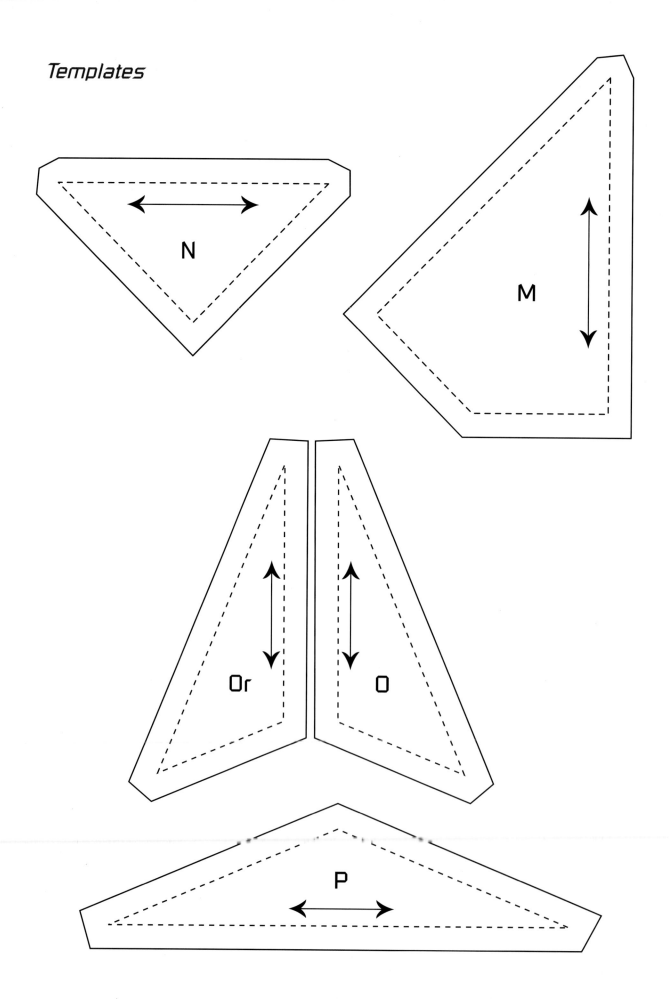

Template K

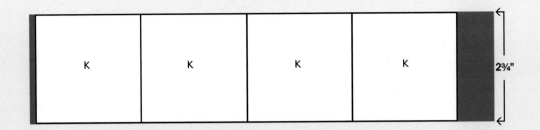

2¾"

Template L

**Note: To center and cut out a special motif,
cut your fabric strips in a single layer, and position the
template on top of the design you wish to feature.**

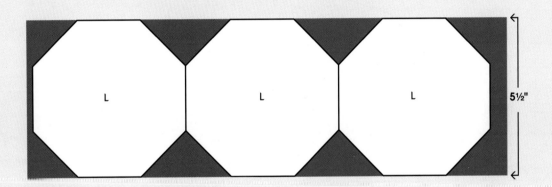

5½"

Template M

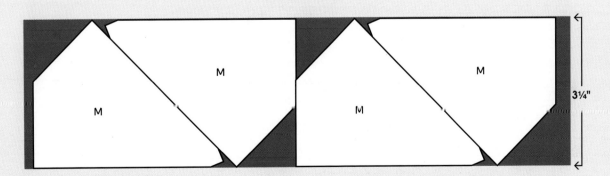

3¼"

Templates

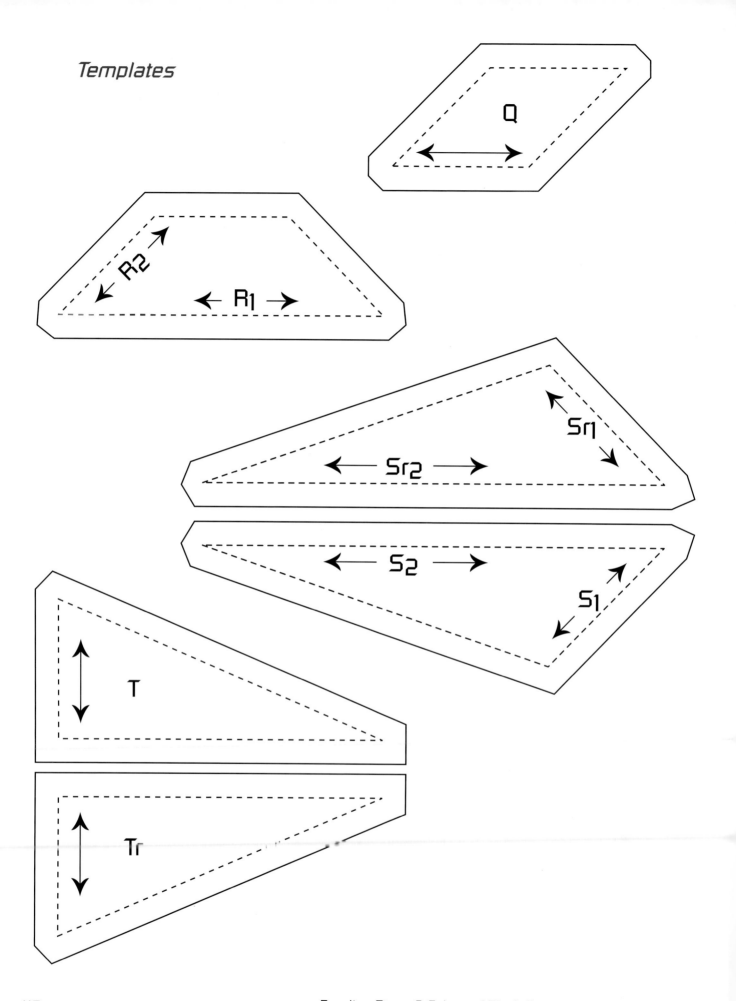

Template N

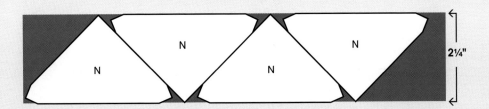

2¼"

Template O

Cutting Template O from a folded strip of fabric will give you an equal number of O and Or pieces.

1¾"

Template P

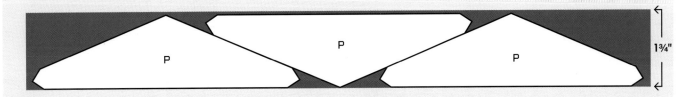

1¾"

Template Q

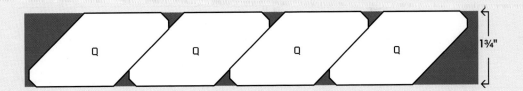

1¾"

Templates

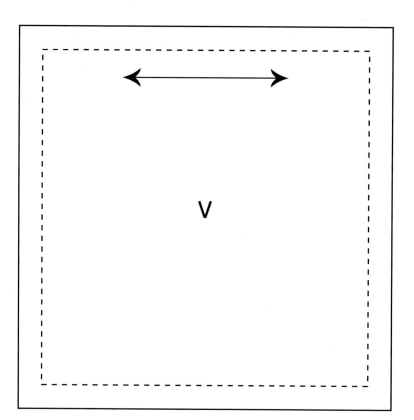

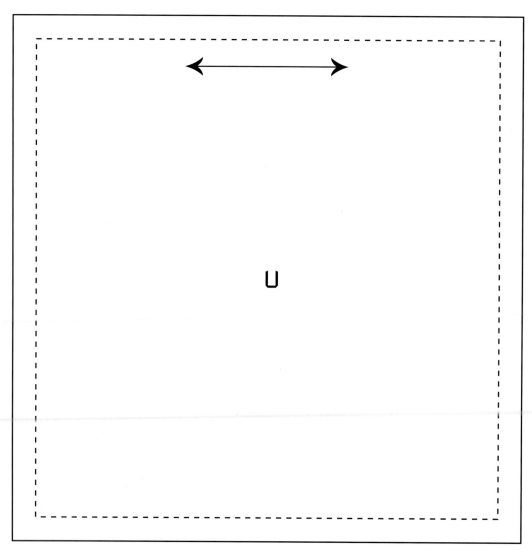

Dazzling Stars: A Galaxy of Block Patterns — Parlato & Stuart

Template R₁

1¾"

Template R₂

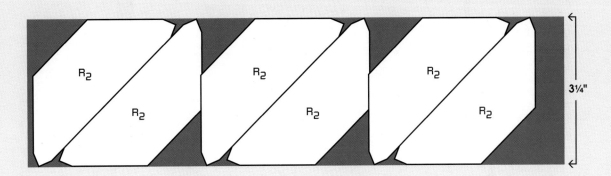

3¼"

Template S₁

Cutting Template S₁ or S₂ from a folded strip
of fabric will give you an equal number
of S₁ and Sr₁ or S₂ and Sr₂ pieces.

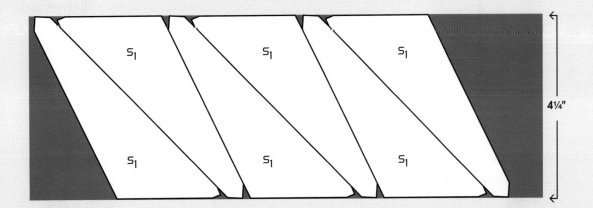

4¼"

Template S₂

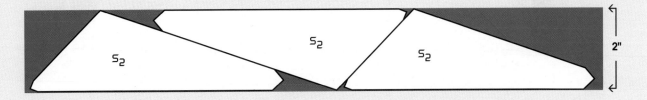

2"

Cutting Diagrams

Template T

Cutting Template T from a folded strip of fabric
will give you an equal number of T and Tr pieces.

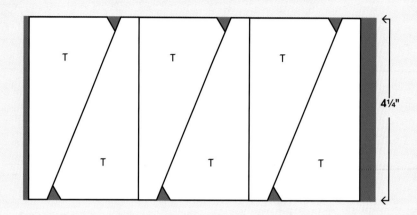

4¼"

Template U

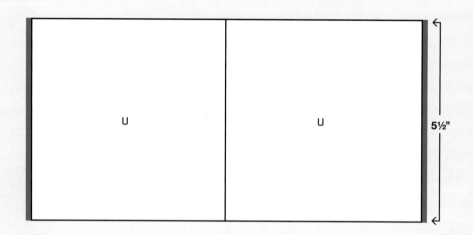

5½"

Template V

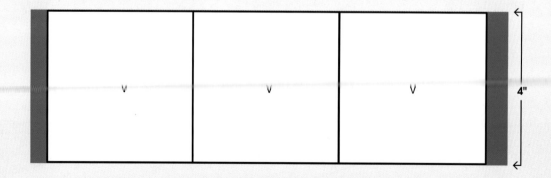

4"

To plan a Dazzling Star quilt, start by determining which fabric you plan to use for each shape in your blocks and the total number of pieces you will need to cut using each template. Depending on the actual widths of your fabrics after they are washed and dried and whether you are using fat quarters or traditional quarter yards, you may get a higher or lower number of pieces from your fabrics. As you calculate the yardages for your quilt, take into account that if you are working with a shape that needs to be cut from a fabric strip wider than 4½", there will be extra fabric leftover in a 9"-wide quarter yard of fabric. Also, when planning to cut a piece of fabric to center a specific motif within a shape, you will need to purchase extra fabric for that template.

Tip: If you like gadgets, a great tool to have for rotary cutting is a rotary turntable. The table spins so that you can stay in one position and still cut around all the sides of your template. This is especially helpful when cutting out L octagons.

The following chart lists the approximate number of pieces that can be cut from a quarter-yard of fabric. Use this information as a starting point for calculating the total amount of yardage you will need for each fabric in your quilt.

Template	Pieces per ¼ yard of fabric
A1	26
A2	32
B	60
C	40
D/Dr	48
E	24
F1	96
F2	102
G1/Gr1	48
G2/Gr2	28
H1	96
H2	102
I1	32
I2	36
J	48
K	45

Template	Pieces per ¼ yard of fabric
L	7*
M	28
N	38
O/Or	70
P	60
Q	75
R1	60
R2	48
S1/Sr1	24
S2/Sr2	52
T/Tr	56
U	7**
V	20

* 9 pieces of Template L can be cut from a fat quarter (18" x 21").

** 9 U center squares can be cut from a fat quarter.

Piecing Guidelines

Many of the units are interchangeable from block to block, which means that you can mix and match the units to create your own, original star designs. The following tips will ensure accurate machine piecing results.

The templates in the previous chapter are specially designed to be easy to sew into rectangular and square units. The same templates will always be sewn to the same partners; all you need to do is refere to the following Piecing Diagrams to be able to piece any of the 48 Dazzling Star blocks in this book.

Accurate Seam Allowances

All of the templates in this book include accurate ¼" seam allowances. It is a good idea to use a patchwork foot (or ¼" presser foot) on your sewing machine to be sure that your seam allowances are consistently the correct width. If you don't have this type of presser foot, try inserting an old needle into your sewing machine and use ¼" graph paper to sew some practice seams. When you have established where an accurate ¼" seam allowance falls on the throat plate of your sewing machine, cut a strip of masking tape and place it at exactly that spot as a guide. (Remember to replace the "practice" needle with a sharp, new one when you start sewing your fabric.)

Tip: One of the best kept secrets of perfect piecing is the use of spray starch. After you've pre-washed and dried your fabrics, spray them lightly with spray starch and press them before you start cutting. The starch will add a little extra stability to your fabric, and you'll be able to cut them more accurately, because they won't slide around on your cutting mat. You'll also be able to sew them with greater precision, because the pieces will tend to stay aligned as they pass under the presser foot.

General Block Construction

Each of the Dazzling Star blocks on pages 18–31 consists of nine units: 4 corner units, 4 side units, and 1 center unit. The piecing order is the same as for a simple nine-patch block. Note: The only exceptions to this piecing sequence are Dazzling Star blocks #43 through #48. These blocks are pieced "in-the-round," as shown under Spiral Construction on page 57.

Step 1
Assemble the smallest sections of each unit.

Step 2
Sew the sections together to create nine units.

Step 3
To complete the block, sew the nine units together in rows of three units each.

Tip: As you sew, place any pieces with bias edges on the bottom, and let the feed dogs do the work of moving it under your needle. This will allow you to sew it without any stretching.

Piecing Diagrams

Sometimes a picture truly is worth a thousand words. The following diagrams show how to piece the different types of units featured in the Dazzling Star blocks on pages 18–33. The arrow on each piece shows the direction the straight grain of the fabric should be positioned. If you are new to quilting and feel a need for more detailed piecing instructions, search out some basic quilting books from quilting friends or your local bookstore.

A Units

Template A is a basic triangle that is used in all three types of units (side, center, and corner) of the Dazzling Star blocks. You can also use this template shape to check your accuracy as you assemble some of the following pieced units. The difference between Template A1 and A2 is simply in the way the template is placed on the grain line of the fabric strip.

To create a center unit, sew two pairs of A1 triangles along one short side, as shown. Press these seam allowances in opposite directions, so that they will fit 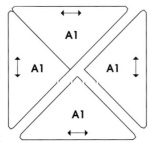 together neatly when the center unit is complete. Then sew the pairs of triangles together, matching seam lines, to form a square. This square should measure 5½", including seam allowances.

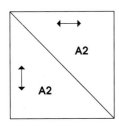 To create a corner unit like this one, join two A2 shapes along their longest sides. The resulting square should measure 4", including seam allowances.

B/C Units

Sew the short sides of two C triangles to the long sides of one B shape. Handle the pieces carefully to avoid distorting the fabric, and make sure that the straight-of-grain in each of your C pieces stays consistent with the way the grain line arrows are shown in the line drawing for the block you are making. Press the seam allowances toward C. Compare the shape of this completed unit to Template A for accuracy.

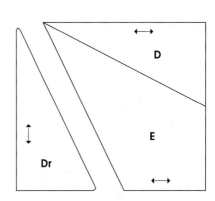

D/E/D(r) Units

For this type of unit, sew the long side of one D and one D(r) to the long sides of one E shape. Press the seam allowances 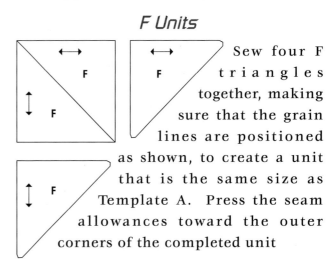 toward D. This pieced unit should measure 4", including seam allowances. (Caution: Templates D and T are very similar in size and shape, so make sure to choose your templates carefully.)

F Units

Sew four F triangles together, making sure that the grain lines are positioned as shown, to create a unit that is the same size as Template A. Press the seam allowances toward the outer corners of the completed unit

G/K/G(r) Units

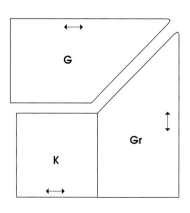

This type of unit features what is often called a "Y" seam, where a third shape is inserted into an angle created by the first two shapes. To piece a unit like this one, start by sewing the short side of the G(r) shape to one side of a K square, stopping this seam exactly ¼" in from the edge of the fabric. Then sew the G shape to the adjacent side of the K square, starting at the outer edge and stopping exactly where the seams intersect. Press these seams toward the G shapes. Finally, sew the angled seam joining the G and G(r) pieces, beginning at the seam intersection at the corner of the K square, and sewing toward the outer corner of the square. This pieced unit should be the same size as Template V.

Tip: When sewing three pieces together in a "Y"-configuration, it is easier to over sew slightly past the ¼" point where the three seam lines intersect, and have to pick out a stitch or two later, than having to go back later and add a stitch or two if there is a gap. To make this easier, don't backstitch at the end of each seam line.

H/I Units

Join the long side of an H1 triangle to the short side of an I shape, and press the seam allowance toward the I. Check this pieced unit against Template A for accuracy.

H/J Units

Join the long sides of an H1 triangle and an H2 triangle to both sides of one point of a J shape for this type of unit. Press the seam allowances toward the H1 and H2 shapes. This pieced unit should be the same size as Template M.

H/L Units

Sew the long sides of two H triangles to the four bias edges of the L octagon, forming a square. Press the seam allowances toward the H triangles. This square should be the same size as Template U.

Template M

This shape is the main star point in many of the Dazzling Star blocks. In other blocks, this same star-point shape is created by piecing other shapes together, such as the H/J unit.

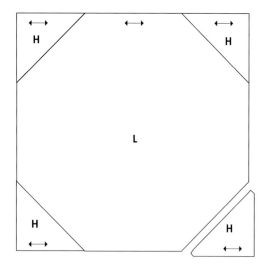

M/A Units

To piece an M/A unit, sew one of the right-angle sides of an A1 triangle to one of the long sides of an M piece. Press the seam allowance toward the M piece.

M/H Unit

Sew one of the right-angle sides of an H1 triangle to one of the short sides of an M piece. Press the seam allowance toward the M piece.

M/A-M/H Units

These two small pieced sections will combine to form a side unit for a Dazzling Star block. Sew an A1 triangle to an M piece, and an M piece to an H1 triangle, and press the seam allowances in opposite directions, so they will fit together nicely when you sew the two sections together to create the rectangular unit. This completed rectangular unit should measure 4" x 5½" including seam allowances.

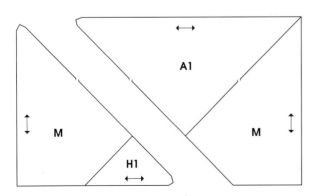

N/G Unit

For this type of unit, sew the short side of a G piece to a short side of an N triangle, matching right angles. Press the seam allowance toward the G piece. This pieced unit should be the same as Template A.

O/P/O(r) Units

This unit is a "Y" construction, where a third piece is inserted into the angle between the first two pieces. Start by sewing the *short* sides of an O(r) and an O piece together, starting from the nubbed corner and stopping ¼" from the opposite end. Press seam to one side.

Gently set-in P at the v-shaped bottom of the joined Os. Start by sewing from the center O seam to one of the outer nubbed corners of P. Repeat with the other side P. Completed triangle should be the same size as Template A.

O/Q/O(r) Units

For this type of unit, sew the *medium-length* sides of pieces O(r) and O together, starting from the nubbed corners and stopping ¼" from the opposite end. Press seam to one side.

Gently set-in Q at the v-shaped bottom of the joined Os. Start by sewing from the center O seam to one of the outer nubbed corners of Q. Repeat with the other side Q. The completed triangle should be the same size as Template M.

O/O(r)/R Units

Sew the *medium-length* sides of an O(r) and an O piece together, starting at the nubbed corner and ending ¼" in from the opposite end. This will form a narrow "V" shape. Press this seam to one side. Gently set in an R1 piece (the short *middle* edge and the *angled right* edge, as shown) between the O and O(r) pieces; start sewing from the seam at the center, working outward toward the edge of the R1 piece.

Repeat to set in the other edge of the R1 piece. Press this seam allowance toward the O and O(r) pieces. This completed unit should match Template A

R/H/R Units

Sew the short middle side of an R1 piece to a short side of an H2 piece, starting at the nubbed corner of H2 and stopping ¼" in from the opposite point. Press this seam to one side. Gently set in an R1 piece, by sewing the left side of an R1 piece to the angled right side of the other R1 piece, starting at the seam where the R1 and H2 pieces meet and sewing outward.

Then join the remaining side of H2 to R1, starting at the seam line and sewing to the other end. Press this seam allowance toward the R1 pieces. This completed unit should match Template A.

R/H/Q Units

Sew the short middle side of an R2 piece to an H1 piece, starting at the outside edge and end-

ing the seam ¼" in from the opposite end. Press this seam to one side. Gently set in a Q piece by placing one side of Q against the remaining short side of H and sewing from center seam outward toward the nubbed corner of Q on one side. Repeat for the other side of Q and the R2 piece, again sewing from the center out. This completed unit should match Template M.

S/D Units

Sew the medium-length side of an S1 piece to the long side of a D triangle. Press the seam allowance toward S1. This completed unit should match Template M.

T/T(r)Units

Sew the long edge of a T(r) piece to a T piece. Press this seam allowance toward the T piece. This completed unit should match Template M.

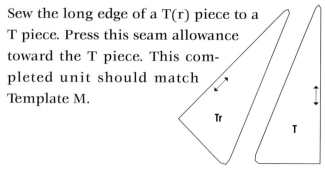

Template U

Template U is a square that measures 5½" including seam allowances.

Template V

Template V is a square that measures 4" including seam allowance.

Spiral Construction

Dazzling Star blocks #43 through #48 are assembled in a slightly different manner than the other blocks. Follow these steps to piece any block with this type of spiral construction.

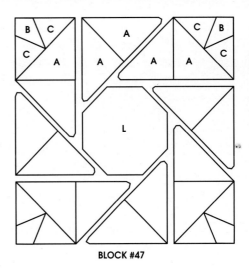

BLOCK #47

Step 1

After you have pieced the main units of one of these blocks, lay the units out on a flat surface, as they will appear in the finished block. Sew the A triangles to the adjoining A triangles or corner unit, creating eight spiral units, as shown.

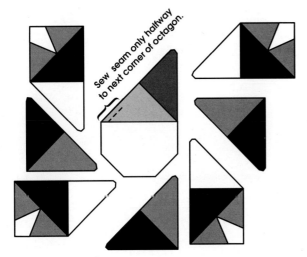

Step 2

Sew the first partial seam, starting at the nubbed corner of the first pair of A triangles, and sewing only *one half of the seam*, as shown. Press this seam allowance toward the L octagon.

Step 3

Moving in a counter-clockwise direction, sew the second spiral unit to the long side of the A triangle and one side of the L octagon, crossing the first partial seam, as shown.

Step 4

Referring to the previous diagram, continue sewing spiral units to the center L octagon in order, as shown, until the last spiral unit is added, completing the block.

Step 5

After the last spiral unit is attached to the L octagon, sew the partial seam you started in to complete the block.

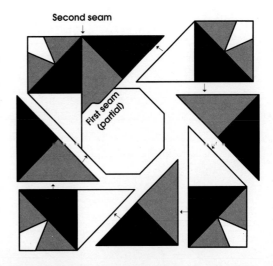

Gallery of Dazzling Star Quilts

The design potential for Dazzling Star blocks is nearly limitless, from antique and traditional to innovative and contemporary. Let the quilts on the following pages inspire your own heavenly creations.

ORDER AND CHAOS

33" x 33". Pieced and machine quilted by Carleen Parlato, Miami, Florida.

This quilt was selected as part of the Hoffman Challenge National Tour, Collection A, 1992. The challenge's theme fabric is featured in the center and background in Dazzling Star blocks #37 and #37 (reversed). Hand-dyed fabrics in strong, bright colors create a dominant, dimensional star. Blue lamé and gold metallic quilting add sparkle. Diagonal squares between the octagonal stars are precision-cut to allow the green blade motif to twirl in the center position.

DREAM STARS
AUDITIONS #1

31" x 31". Pieced by Carleen Parlato. Machine quilted by Harriet Rudoff, Miami, Florida.

This quilt is the first in a series of samples exploring the effect of color and value placement. This quilt features Dazzling Star blocks #16, #23, #12, and #3 (clockwise, starting with the block with the bird in the center).

DREAM STARS
AUDITIONS #2

31" x 31". Pieced by Carleen Parlato. Machine quilted by Harriet Rudoff, Miami, Florida.

This quilt shows Dazzling Star block #10 with rotated corners, as well as blocks #16, #4, and #11, shown clockwise starting with the star with the pink background.

DAZZLING DREAMSTAR SAMPLER

31" x 31". Pieced by Carleen Parlato. Machine quilted by Harriet Rudoff, Miami, Florida.

Two of the blocks in this wallhanging feature large floral centers, while the other two have centers that make the stars appear to "float" in the design. Carleen used Dazzling Star blocks #34, #48 (reversed), #46, and #43, with corner and side variations from Dazzling Star block #41.

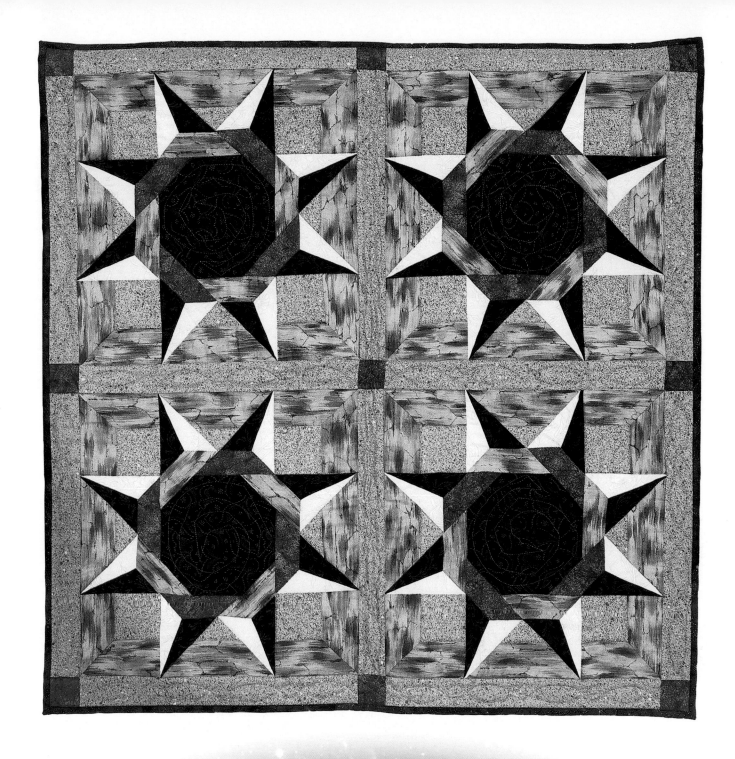

RIBBON STAR

28¾" x 28¾". Pieced and machine quilted by Carleen Parlato, Miami, Florida.

In this four-block wallhanging, two stars are constructed exactly as the templates for the Dazzling Star blocks indicate, while the other two blocks have their star points reversed. The brush-stroke fabric adds a soft, linear component to the center ribbon and outside frame of the block.

SLINGS AND ARROWS

28" x 28". Pieced and machine quilted by Carleen Parlato, Miami, Florida.

These four stars feature Dazzling Star blocks #41 and #41 reversed. The linear fabric in the outside "S" shapes creates a motif that seems to flow, producing an outline around the stars.

DAZZLING FIREWORKS

31½" x 31½". Pieced by Carleen Parlato. Machine quilted by Harriet Rudoff, Miami, Florida.

These stars originally started out with a large floral fabric in their centers, but when Carleen discovered that the red and white star points looked just like fireworks, she replaced the floral with actual fireworks fabric, creating a very exciting quilt! The rotation of the corner units creates even more explosions of color in a secondary design. Carleen used Dazzling Star block #9, with a corner variation from block #39 for this quilt.

CACTUS FLOWER

30" x 30". Pieced and machine quilted by Carleen Parlato, Miami, Florida.

A bright Southwestern fabric was the inspiration for this quilt. By precision-cutting various repeat motifs in the fabric, Carleen created a quilt that shows off a variety of floral centers, using Dazzling Star block #22.

THE AMERICAN DREAM

32" x 30" flag; 2" diameter x 35" flag pole. Pieced and machine quilted by Carleen Parlato, Miami, Florida.

An American flag challenge by her local quilting guild inspired Carleen to make this quilt which uses a single Dazzling Star block #43. A variety of striped fabrics gives the secondary star points additional radiance.

STARS AT A CROSSROAD

29" x 29". Pieced and machine quilted by Carleen Parlato, Miami, Florida.

Carleen used an unusual stripe to accentuate the linear aspect of Dazzling Star block #8. She also used hand-dyed and hand-marbled fabrics in the star points. The angles of the "crossroads" are continued into the border to complete the design.

KALEIDOSCOPE
IN THE GARDEN

41" x 41". Pieced by Carleen Parlato. Machine quilted by Harriet Rudoff, Miami, Florida.

Carleen first picked Dazzling Star block #19, then chose fabric that would enhance the design of this quilt. She created a modified kaleidoscope effect by precision-cutting the four center triangles from the same motif in the fabric. To try this easy effect yourself, see page 14.

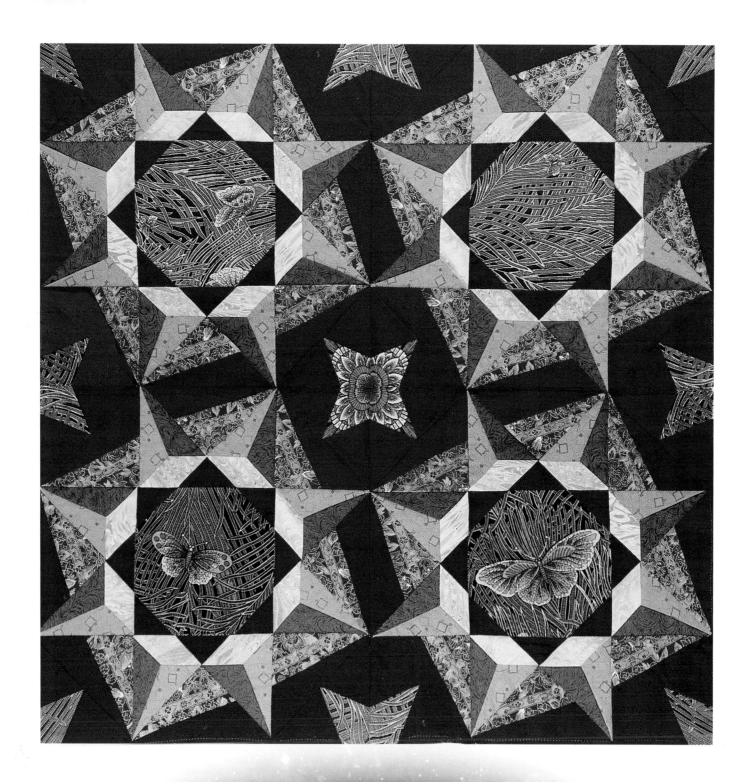

BUTTERFLY IN THE GARDEN

28" x 28". Pieced and machine quilted by Carleen Parlato, Miami, Florida.

The fabric chosen for the center of Dazzling Star block #37 sets the tone for all the other fabrics in this dramatic wallhanging. All of the blocks were cut identically, so that all of the off-angle background blocks would go in the same direction. Compare this design to SLINGS AND ARROWS, page 64, where two of the four blocks are reversed.

TREE TALK?
BACKYARD GOSSIP

33¼" x 33¼". Pieced and machine quilted by Liana Miller, Miami, Florida.

The large open center in Dazzling Star block #41 was perfect for playing up the bright rainforest fabric in this quilt. Liana adapted the block to create a fifth "block" in the center of the quilt, to showcase more of the rainforest's inhabitants.

CITYSCAPE

37" x 44½". Pieced and machine quilted by Janet McIntyre, Miami, Florida.

Janet says she likes abstract design. "That's why my quilt doesn't look like stars. I like people to see something they don't expect." She used Dazzling Star block #25 and was inspired to name her quilt "Cityscape" because the overall effect was very architectural. "To me it looked like gray buildings up against a blue sky," she said.

STARS ON THE WEB.COM

30½" x 30½". Pieced and machine quilted by LaVerne Johnson, Miami, Florida.

LaVerne says that her inspiration for this quilt came from the center Hoffman fabric. "The first people who looked at the fabric said it looked like an umbrella. Then, others thought it looked like a spider-web." A daily Internet user, LaVerne loves to explore quilt sites on the Web. She used Dazzling Star block #18 in this quilt.

CRYSTAL STAR

32½" x 32½" . Pieced by Ann L. Mitchell. Machine quilted by Harriet Rudoff, Miami, Florida.

Ann used a computer to help design this quilt. She chose Dazzling Star block #36, one of the more dynamic designs in this book, and put the pattern into QuiltPro to see how each color worked in each position in the star. Harriet machine quilted in gold metallic thread to emphasize the subtle glitter of the main fabric.

STARRY NIGHT

31¼" x 31¼". Pieced and machine quilted by Janet Swan, Miami, Florida.

To make this quilt, Janet started in the center and worked her way out. "First, I chose the star I wanted to make. Then I remembered an interesting, dark, pebbly fabric I had. I hadn't used it in a quilt yet. When I saw this star, I thought it would be great for the center. I chose the rest of the fabrics based on that." Janet adds that her quilt got its name because it reminded her of a nighttime sky. She used Dazzling Star block #1 and machine pieced and quilted her quilt.

RADIATION

31½" x 31½". Pieced and machine quilted by Louise E. Regan, Miami, Florida.

Louise's inspiration for her quilt came from the fabrics she selected. "Once I had combined the different fabrics with the block print, I knew I wanted to create a radiating bull's-eye effect. This pattern and the selected palette of fabrics helped me accomplish this." Louise used Dazzling Star block #4 and machine pieced and quilted this wallhanging.

Dazzling Stars: A Galaxy of Block Patterns – Parlato & Stuart

MONDAY NIGHT STARS II

31" x 31". Pieced and machine quilted by Peggy Dolaway Schemenauer, Miami, Florida.

The A templates, which are in the center and circle the Dazzling Star block #24, are ideal for featuring stripes or border prints. "When you don't have a striped fabric readily available, you can create your own. In this quilt, most of the A triangles are cut from fabric I strip-pieced together. The visual focus of each block is affected by the placement of color." Peggy machine pieced and quilted this quilt.

LATE BLOOMERS

45" x 45". Pieced and hand quilted by Peggy Dolaway Schemenauer, Miami, Florida.

Peggy noticed that Dazzling Star block #16 resembled a flower when it was viewed on-point. She cut out her flower center from fabrics with large roses in them and enhanced the floral feeling by hand quilting vines and leaves in the sashing, using variegated thread and the BigStitch method. The dark background fabric inspired her to add the stars and moons.

WISH UPON A SEA OF STARS

59" x 59". Pieced and hand quilted by Mary DeWind, Miami, Florida.

Mary used Dazzling Star block #23 and selected an assortment of Jinny Beyer millennium fabrics with the idea of making something memorable. The gold fabric is a Kona Bay design, and the alternate blocks and side triangles feature a Hoffman batik. Once she started making the stars and discovered how easy and rewarding they were to piece, she says, "I just couldn't stop!"

NEUTRAL ZONE

59" x 72". Designed and pieced by Jane Hardy Miller. Machine quilted by Harriet Rudoff, Miami, Florida.

Jane used many different Dazzling Star blocks for this quilt, setting them against a variety of smaller stars. "I don't like to make the same block over and over; I don't find it as interesting," she explains. "The warm millennium fabric came into the store, and then I found another colorway. I kept on searching until I found a third colorway, which I overdyed. I thought this would be a good reminder of the year in which I made the quilt."

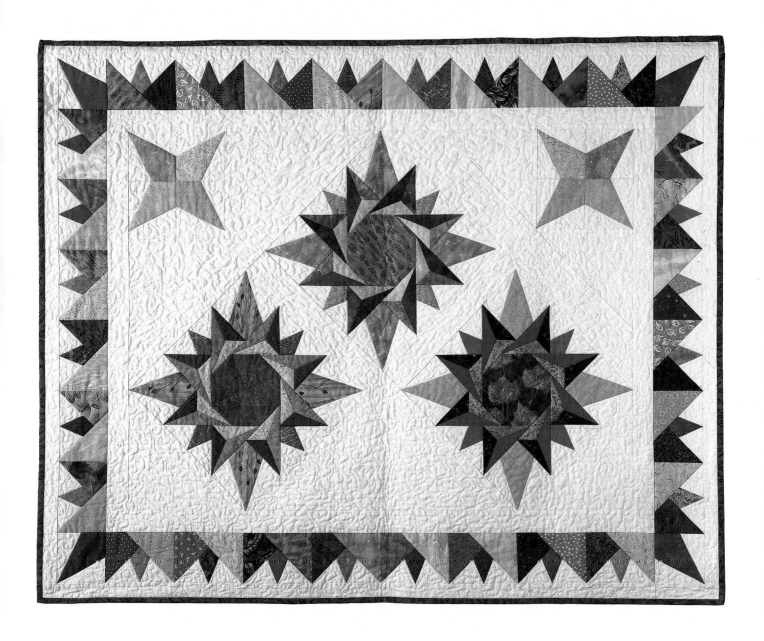

SPARKLERS

49" x 39". Pieced and machine quilted by Patricia Helmcamp, Miami, Florida.

Patricia chose to use Dazzling Star block #43 because she liked the octagon in the center of that design. She also used templates D and E to create a secondary pattern of two smaller stars. She constructed the intriguing border in this quilt using templates A, B, C, and M.

STARS — TRADING COLORS

23¾" x 23¾". Pieced and machine quilted by Phyllis S. Salt, Miami, Florida.

Phyllis used Dazzling Star block #46 to make this striking wallhanging. To make the four-block design more of a challenge, she rotated the colors of the pieces in each block, giving every star a completely different dimension, yet providing overall unity to the quilt. Notice how the placement of darks and lights makes some stars appear to "spin" to the right, while others appear to "spin" to the left.

Dazzling Stars: A Galaxy of Block Patterns – Parlato & Stuart

WISHING ON A DAZZLING STAR

50" x 60". Pieced and machine quilted by Alberta Dalke, Miami, Florida.

Alberta made this quilt to honor the birth of her first granddaughter. She incorporated more than 150 different fabrics, many of which have space and sky motifs. She decided on Dazzling Star block #11 and rotated the corner units to shine the light on her original appliqué of a young girl gazing toward the future. Her quilting designs emphasize the rays of light, and she included phrases from childhood songs along the border.

HALLOWEEN STAR

34" x 34". Pieced and machine quilted by Alberta Dalke, Miami, Florida.

After finishing WISHING ON A DAZZLING STAR, Alberta decided to make another quilt on the spur of the moment. She used a set of fat quarters with a Halloween theme to get started, and then added additional fabrics to complete the quilt which features, appropriately enough, Dazzling Star block #13!

FIRE STARS

32½" x 32½". Pieced by Martha G. Sussenberger.
Machine quilted by Jacquelyn L. Rowe, Homestead, Florida.

Martha says that the block she chose for her quilt, Dazzling Star block #21, was not at all difficult to put together – once she made her final color choices! "Making the block didn't take any time at all, but deciding on the fabrics took me about four months!"

CHILES FLAMBÉ

39" x 38½". Pieced by Diane Powers Harris. Machine quilted by Jacquelyn L. Rowe, Miami, Florida.

Inspired by a recent purchase of chile basket fabric, Diane also included several other chile fabrics. She lavishly embellished her wallhanging with approximately 350 size 6mm pearls, chile buttons, blown glass chiles, and manipulated ribbon. The body of the quilt is stitched-in-the-ditch, while the border features thread painting to create the dancing chiles. Heavy outline quilting in the corner chiles gives added emphasis. Diane used Dazzling Star block #3 for her quilt.

TRANSATLANTIC SCRAPS

37½" x 37½". Pieced by Jo Walters. Machine quilted by Harriet Rudoff, Miami, Florida.

At the 1989 Quilts U.K. Exhibit in England, Jo met Katherine Guerrier, one of Britain's top quiltmakers. An exchange of creative ideas was immediately begun, and some years and many letters later, the two quiltmakers began sending each other fabrics, especially batiks. Many of those fabrics are featured in the Dazzling Star block #7 in this quilt.

STARS OF WONDER

65" x 65". Pieced by Victoria Stuart. Machine quilted by Harriet Rudoff, Miami, Florida.

As soon as she saw the new cotton-rayon "lamé" fabrics in Christmas red and green, Victoria knew they would be perfect for the braided ribbon around the center of Dazzling Star block #48. She set the stars on-point and used plain setting squares. Harriet quilted a gorgeous, sparkling poinsettia motif in the borders, which makes this a perfect holiday wall quilt.

PORCELAIN MOSAIC

51" x 51". Pieced by Victoria Stuart. Machine quilted by Harriet Rudoff, Miami, Florida.

For the main fabric in this quilt, Victoria chose a large flower print that reminded her of antique porcelain china. She combined Dazzling Star block #11 and the corner unit from Dazzling Star block #9 to create an interesting secondary pattern. Harriet quilted a beautiful feathered border and corners and did lots of stipple quilting to enhance the fragile porcelain look.

SCOTCH BROTH

61½" x 63½". Pieced by Victoria Stuart. Machine quilted by Harriet Rudoff, Miami, Florida.

To minimize the scrappiness of this quilt, Victoria used a dominant central block and repeated blocks of the same color in opposing positions. Her Dazzling Star #41 blocks are set on-point, side-by-side, which makes them appear to spin. Harriet's overall star quilting pattern enhances this effect and unifies the whole design.

Dazzling Stars: A Galaxy of Block Patterns — Parlato & Stuart

ORIENTAL EXPRESSIONS

35" x 35". Pieced by Victoria Stuart. Machine quilted by Harriet Rudoff, Miami, Florida.

The inspiration for this little quilt was a fat-quarter collection of Oriental fabrics. Victoria used the feature fabric for the centers of the Dazzling Star #11 blocks, and added various blues and reds in the same positions in each block. The reverse side of one of the star point fabrics is used in the inner border, and Harriet's machine quilting features a lovely floral motif that was inspired by the designs on the Chinese vases.

WINDSWEPT GARDEN

51" x 51". Pieced by Victoria Stuart. Machine quilted by Harriet Rudoff, Miami, Florida.

Victoria chose Dazzling Star block #45 to set off a floral print, and pastel pinks and blues as the ribbons and star points. Her mother, Joan, came up with the idea of adding the tiny, dark blue border around each block and using a straight set with blue and yellow sashing. Harriet quilted flowing leaves in the sashing, tiny leafy vines in the pink ribbons, and a Miami Beach Art Deco-inspired design in the border.

LITTLE RAYS OF SUNSHINE

20" x 48". Pieced by Victoria Stuart. Machine quilted by Harriet Rudoff, Miami, Florida.

Sunflowers on the label of a shampoo bottle inspired this quilt. Victoria used bright, high-contrast colors in Dazzling Star block #46 to create a feeling of visual depth in the "flower." She chose Corner Variation #6 in the sashing to create the effect of large sunflower leaves.

STAR #1

36" x 36". Pieced and machine quilted by Harriet Rudoff, Miami, Florida.

Harriet was given the challenge by her quilt guild, Ocean Waves, NQA, to use this blue and yellow stained glass fabric in a 36" square quilt. "It was a difficult challenge until I decided to use one of the Dazzling Star blocks (#19) for the design. I chose several bright fabrics to go with the stained glass fabric, but it still needed something more. It all came together when I added the appliqué vine." Harriet machine quilted freehand to enhance some of the designs of the fabrics.

EYE OF THE STAR

36⅜" x 36⅜". Pieced and machine quilted by Diane Powers Harris, Miami, Florida.

Diane made this quilt for the Phyllis Solakian Memorial Quilt Challenge for the Ocean Waves annual quilt show QuiltFest 2000. The challenge was to create a 36" square wallhanging using four 12" blocks as well as using a recognizable amount (up to a half-yard) of the challenge fabric, seen here in the center octagons. Diane used Dazzling Star block #46 in her quilt.

Navigating the Stars:
Planning a Star Quilt

This book is like a constellation of stars! Select any of the Dazzling Star blocks that appeal to you and use these guidelines to create your own special quilts.

Photocopy the Block Diagrams

The shaded diagrams of the Dazzling Star blocks on pages 18–33 will help you come up with intriguing design possibilities for your quilts. Photocopy these diagrams (for personal use only) or scan blocks you like into a computer and experiment with placements of color and value, and explore the potential for secondary designs.

Choose a Setting

After you have determined which blocks you want to include in your quilt, it's time to think about a setting. You can create fields of stars, rows of stars, stars within stars, or just a single star shining in a one-of-a-kind quilt—the possibilities are limitless.

> Do you want your star to be a real stand-out? Consider a straight setting with sashing or alternate blocks of plain fabric in between. Do you prefer the secondary designs to shine? Try placing your blocks side-by-side or on-point.

Guidelines for On-Point Settings

Use the following cutting measurements for the alternate squares and the setting triangles for Dazzling Star blocks set on-point.

Cut alternate squares 12½" x 12½".

For side/setting triangles, start by cutting 21" squares and cut these squares in half diagonally, twice, to get four quarter-square-triangles from each one.

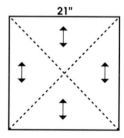

For corner triangles, start by cutting two 14½" squares. Then cut each square diagonally to create four corner triangles.

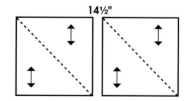

Designing a Dazzling Border

The rectangular units used to make Dazzling Star blocks can
also be used to create exciting and expressive borders for your quilts.
Try combining the units of your star blocks in new ways to add a
dynamite border to your quilt. Here are a few ideas.

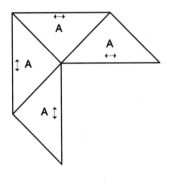

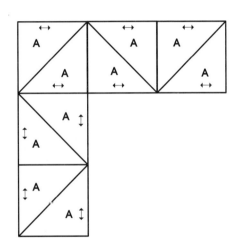

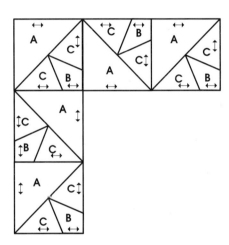

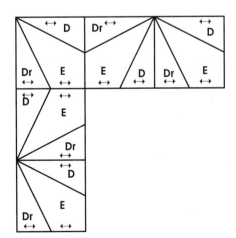

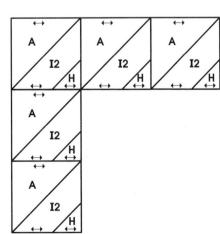

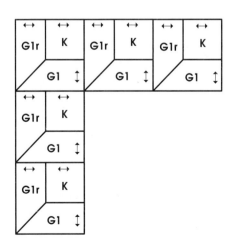

Creative Quilting Patterns

If you love to quilt, whether by hand or machine, Dazzling Star blocks will give you a wide open field to display your talents. The large center areas can be filled with a variety of special motifs, while the star points and secondary designs offer unlimited potential for innovative quilting patterns.

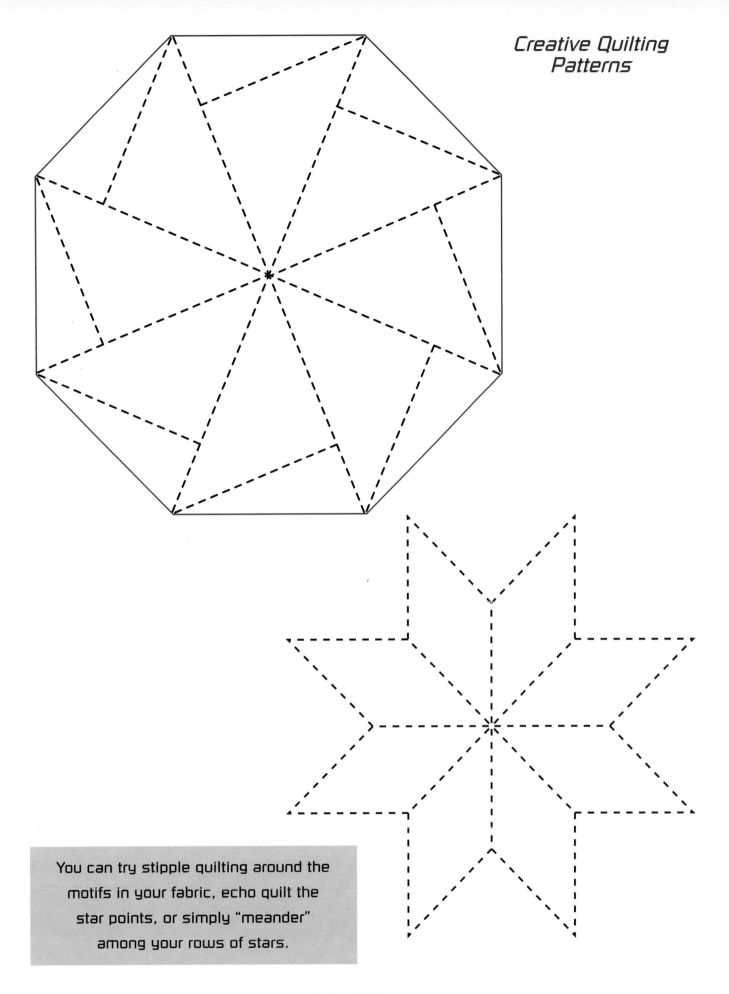

You can try stipple quilting around the motifs in your fabric, echo quilt the star points, or simply "meander" among your rows of stars.

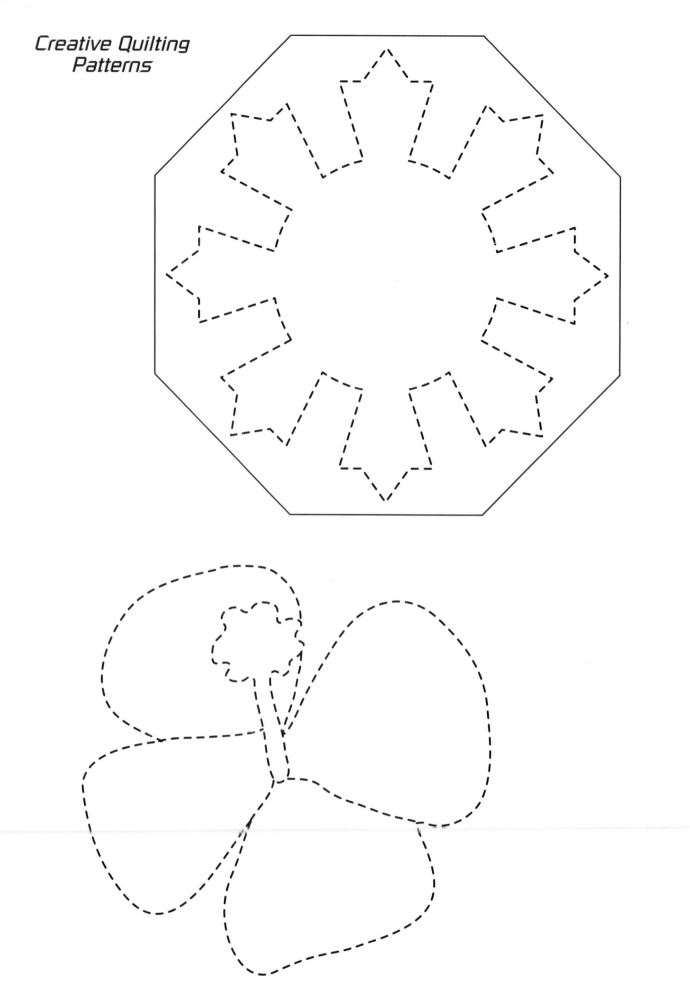

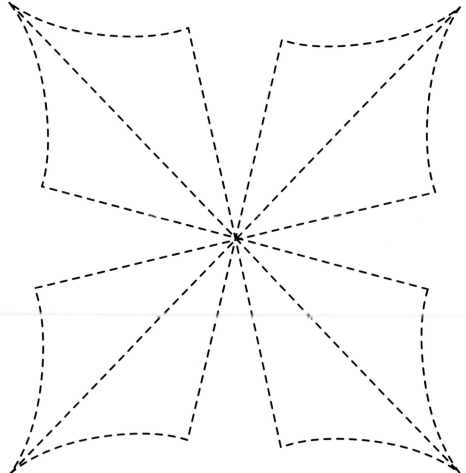

Dazzling Stars: A Galaxy of Block Patterns – Parlato & Stuart

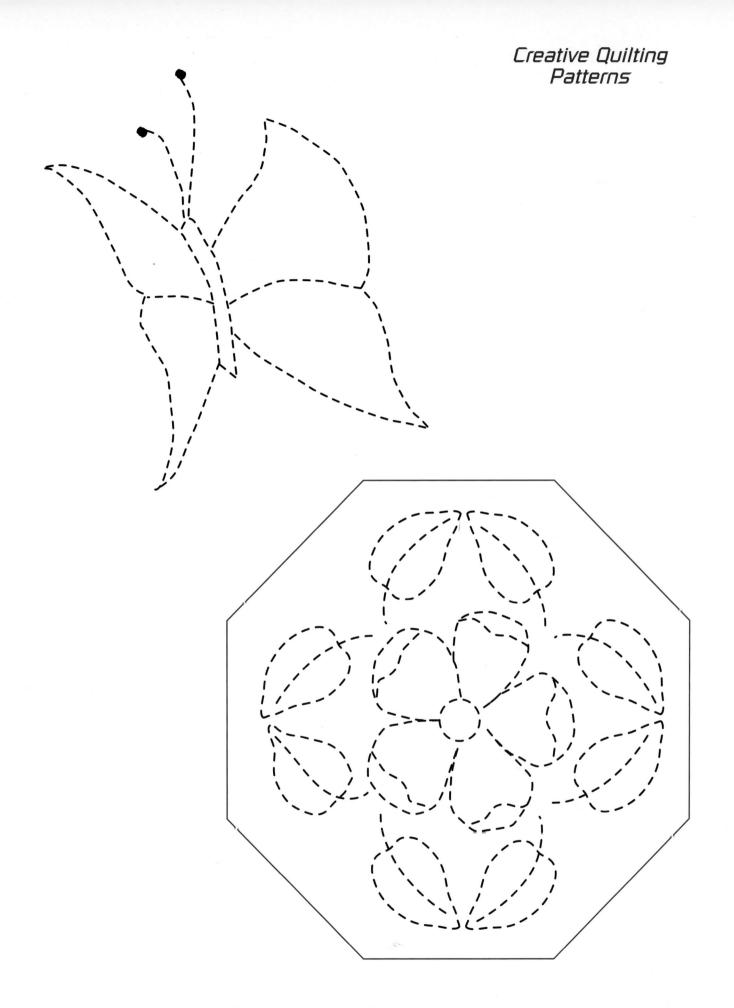

Dazzling Stars: A Galaxy of Block Patterns – Parlato & Stuart

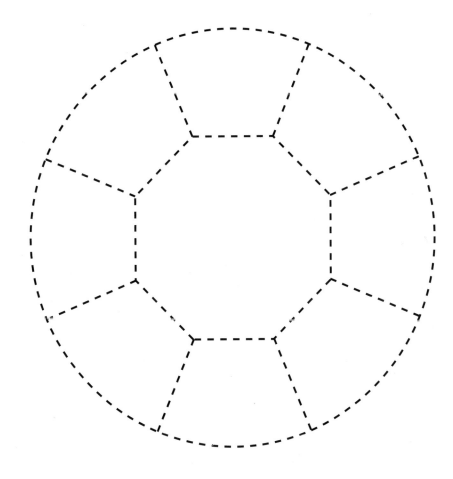

Creative Quilting
Patterns

Contributing Artists

This book would not have been possible without the following quilters who created a magnificent and stunning collection of quilts for the gallery. We are extremely grateful for their enthusiastic participation and extraordinary creativity. Thank you all for letting your light shine!

Alberta Dalke
WISHING ON A DAZZLING STAR (page 83)
and HALLOWEEN STAR (page 84)

A self-taught quilter for more than 20 years, Alberta Dalke is best known for her scrap and multifabric quilts and miniature quilts. Her work has won several awards, including the Viewer's Choice Award for four years in a row at the Ocean Waves NQA annual QuiltFest in Coral Gables, Florida. She has taught quiltmaking classes to Girl Scouts from the inner city, who are some of Alberta's favorite students. A retired registered nurse, Alberta returned to school and earned a Bachelor of Science degree in electrical engineering in 2000.

Mary DeWind
WISH UPON A SEA OF STARS (page 79)

A crime analyst for the Coral Gables Police Department, Mary began quilting seriously in 1988, joining the Ocean Waves Chapter, NQA in 1989. She started exhibiting her work at local quilt shows, winning ribbons for her miniatures, hand appliqué, pieced wallhangings, and wearable art. She has participated in Hoffman Challenges, and her entries were part of the nationwide exhibition. She received an honorable mention for a vest in the amateur fashion show competition at the 1998 International Quilt Festival in Houston, Texas. She has organized several quilting symposiums, including her guild's annual QuiltFest. She is a member of the Ocean Waves Board, serving as president from 1998–1999. She was named Quilter of the Year in 2000.

Diane Powers Harris
CHILES FLAMBÉ (page 86)
EYE OF THE STAR (page 95)

A quiltmaker for more than 20 years, Diane is the founder of the Ocean Waves Chapter, NQA in Miami, Florida. In addition to serving in various areas for the guild, she has chaired the Quilt Escape workshop series, was the director of Quilter's Paradise, and helped to initiate QuiltFest, the guild's annual quilt show and competition. Diane also served on the Florida Quilt Heritage Documentation Project as the area coordinator for Miami-Dade County, and was involved for several years with the annual quilt competition of the Historical Association of Southern Florida as an integral part of the show's hanging and judging process. She was appointed the National Quilting Association's Annual Show Coordinator for 2001.

Patricia Helmcamp
SPARKLERS (page 81)

As a child, Patricia admired the many wonderful quilts her mother, Alma Wooten, made, yet felt that she herself did not have either the time or the ability to quilt. That changed in 1988, however, when her mother underwent major surgery. Patricia spent several weeks with her mother during her recuperation in West Virginia, and, together, they shared their quilting knowledge. Patricia read all of her mother's quilting books, found the time to quilt, and began to understand why her mother enjoyed quilting so much. Patricia is now a prolific and award-winning quilter in her own right.

LaVerne Johnson
STARS ON THE WEB.COM (page 73)

LaVerne is a retired nurse who has enjoyed quilting for more than 15 years. She has served the Ocean Waves Chapter, NQA in several administrative and volunteer capacities, but she says that being the treasurer for the guild's annual QuiltFest is by far her favorite job. LaVerne is an accomplished machine quilter, but her quilting talents are numerous. She has won many awards for her work and has twice been accepted into the Hoffman Challenge. One of her quilts also traveled with an exhibit to Australia for three months. LaVerne is also a skilled needleworker, specializing in canvas work.

Janet McIntyre
CITYSCAPE (page 72)

A quilter for more than 11 years, Janet has always loved quilts and fabric. Her grandmother, who lived with her family during her entire life, was a quilter who enjoyed making postage stamp quilts. Janet specializes in creating contemporary art quilts. Her award-winning work has appeared in such national shows as the American Quilter's Society annual show in Paducah, Kentucky in 1998, as well as in Art Quilt 21 in Lowell, Massachusetts in 2000, among others.

Jane Hardy Miller
Neutral Zone (page 80)

Jane Hardy Miller began quilting in 1968 in California. Until she moved to Miami in 1979, she was a self-taught quiltmaker, figuring out what to do as she went along. Since taking a beginning quilting class at a local quilt shop (and learning about accurate ¼" seams), Jane has made numerous quilts, both traditional and innovative in style. She was named Quilter of the Year of the Ocean Waves Chapter, NQA in 1992, and has won numerous top awards for her quilts at major shows throughout the country. Her pieces have also been featured in several art and quilting magazines.

Liana Miller
Tree Talk? Backyard Gossip (page 71)

Liana's first quiltmaking teacher more than 18 years ago was Irene McLaren, who really encouraged her. Liana went on to become a founding member of her local guild, the Ocean Waves Chapter, NQA, serving in many capacities, including historian, membership chair, and organizer of the guild's annual QuiltFest. Best known for her use of bright fabrics and bold colors in innovative designs, Liana has made many award-winning quilts, one of which was selected for the Hoffman Challenge in 1998. She also has been a volunteer at the International Quilt Festival for several years.

Ann L. Mitchell
Crystal Star (page 74)

Ann started quilting in Pennsylvania in 1985 at a small local shop, and her love of quilting really blossomed after visiting Lancaster, Pennsylvania, and attending the annual Amish quilt sales every July. When she and her husband moved to Miami in 1987, she joined the local guild immediately. Now a member of two small groups and two guilds, she has held a variety of positions, including president. Ann is an avid computer quilter, extending her quilting experience through e-mail and quilting chat rooms, where she has built friendships with quilters from all over the world. She has been featured in news articles and quilting magazines several times.

Louise E. Regan
Radiation (page 76)

Louise Regan has been a quiltmaker and quilt designer for more than 16 years. Originally from Texas, she has lived all over the eastern United States, including Michigan, Maryland, Louisiana, and Florida. These travels have exposed her to a wonderful variety of quilters and quilting styles, and they have also become an inspiring influence in creating her own quilt designs. An award-winning quilter and registered nurse, Louise currently lives in Miami, Florida.

Harriet D. Rudoff
Star #1 (page 94)

A registered nurse for 30 years, Harriet has been a quilter for more than 20 years. In 1999, she opened her own business, Just Quilting Around, Inc., a custom quilting and finishing service. Harriet is an award-winning quilter whose work includes everything from innovative quilts to quilted garments. She is best known for the Oriental flavor of her designs and her use of bold colors. She

was named Quilter of the Year of the Ocean Waves Chapter, NQA in 1996. She has been actively involved in the guild for many years, serving in roles from Membership Chair to President, managing to pull together the annual QuiltFest in the Spring of 1993, just a few months after Hurricane Andrew devastated South Florida.

Phyllis S. Salt
Stars – Trading Colors (page 82)

Phyllis has always been interested in quilting, taking her first quilting class in 1978 with Irene McLaren. She has also taken classes at her local quilt shop, and she joined the Ocean Waves Chapter, NQA in 1992, serving on the board as membership chair, secretary, and president. She retired from her job as secretary at Miami-Dade Community College in 1995, but continues her role in education by teaching beginning quilting classes. Her husband died shortly before the couple celebrated their fiftieth wedding anniversary, and Phyllis says that she manages to keep her sanity thanks to quilting and her quilter friends.

Peggy Dolaway Schemenauer
Monday Night Stars II (page 77) and Late Bloomers (page 78)

Peggy is a prolific and award-winning quilter who is best known for her extraordinary hand appliqué and hand quilting. Her beautiful quilt, BLOOMING LILY FEATHER STAR, won the top three awards in 1992 at The Harvest, the annual quilt competition sponsored by the Historical Association of South Florida: Best of Show, First Place in Mixed Techniques, and People's Choice. Her quilt was featured in the American Quilter's Society 1993 Engagement Calendar for the month of April. Peggy is an active member of the Ocean Waves Chapter, NQA, where she has served as secretary and as the organizer of the group's first QuiltFest. Peggy also belongs to several smaller quilting groups which meet weekly or biweekly to share ideas, techniques, and inspiration . . . and sometimes recipes!

Martha Gutierrez Sussenberger
Fire Stars (page 85)

A quiltmaker for approximately five years, Martha lives in Miami, Florida. She is an active member of several guilds, as well as being a charter member of the Sunshine State Quilters. She has entered many quilt shows, and her quilts have won several awards. Martha is also a quilting entrepreneur, operating My Stash, a source of notions and books geared specifically to quiltmaking. She says that the Dazzling Star project was presented to her with great enthusiasm and that she was a very willing participant.

Janet Swan
Starry Night (page 75)

Janet started quilting in 1982 in Fayetteville, North Carolina, when she signed up for a class in lap quilting. At that time, the class fee was just $5.00, and she became immediately intrigued with the art of quiltmaking. She is active in her local guild, the Ocean Waves Chapter, NQA, where she is a constant volunteer for everything from helping with the Show-and-Tell portion of the meetings, to coordinating the guild's annual quilt show. She makes about five quilts a year, and her pieces have won ribbons at shows in Miami, North Carolina, and Missouri. Most of her quilts are given to family and friends.

Jo Walters
Transatlantic Scraps (page 87)

Among Jo's numerous awards are her prize-winning entries in three AQS shows and three consecutive International Quilt Festival shows, one of which was featured in the AIQA 1992 calendar. Her first quilt, made in 1989, took the award for Best First Quilt at the Great British Quilt Festival. Jo has taught her BigStitch technique throughout the United States, England, and Scotland, as well as at the International Quilt Festival in Houston, Texas. Her quilts and quilting techniques have appeared in many quilt magazines, such as Japan's *Patchwork Quilts Tsu-Shin*, as well as in several quilt books.

Resources

Whenever possible, support your local quilt shop in obtaining supplies mentioned in this book. If you find that the templates recommended and other quiltmaking products are not locally available, the following resources should be able to meet your needs.

Carleen Parlato
12320 SW 109 Terrace
Miami, FL 33186
e-mail: cdparlato@aol.com
Cash or check only
*Template sets and
turntable cutting mats*
*Information on Dazzling Stars classes /
lectures available upon request*

Quilter's Rule International LLC
817 Mohr Avenue
Waterford, WI 53185
Phone: (800) 343-8671
Fax: (877) 714-7853
Web: www.quiltersrule.com
Retail and wholesale;
MasterCard/VISA accepted
General quiltmaking supplies

About the Authors

Photo by Juan E. Cabrera

Carleen Demshok Parlato is a quiltmaker, quilt teacher, and past president of the Ocean Waves (Miami) Chapter of the National Quilting Association.

A beginning quiltmaking class at her local quilt shop first set Carleen on her path to the stars. Since then, she has completed dozens of quilts and won several awards, including Quilter of the Year from the Ocean Waves Chapter of the National Quilting Association. Her Dazzling DreamStar block won the 1992 Fairfield Processing Corporation's "Star Gazing" Quilt Block Contest, and her quilt made of DreamStars, ORDER AND CHAOS, was selected as part of the Hoffman Challenge National Tour in 1992.

Carleen has taught quiltmaking at South Florida quilting guilds, in community schools, in craft stores, and in quilt shops. She has lectured to groups all around her state, and she is well recognized for her commitment to organizing community service projects to create and distribute quilts to orphans, disadvantaged children, and women's shelters.

A nurse practitioner with extensive experience, as well as a wife and mother of two children, Carleen recently fulfilled another goal when she earned a black belt in karate.

Victoria Stuart is an award-winning professional freelance writer. Her articles have been published in *Quilter's Newsletter Magazine*, *Quilting International*, *Quilting Today*, and many others.

Carleen Demshok Parlato was Victoria's first quilting teacher in 1988. "I was the worst student in the class; I didn't even know what a running stitch was! But I got hooked on quilting before we were halfway through the first lesson! Then I attended my first quilt show, and I knew this would become a lifelong passion." Today, Victoria is a quilt teacher for The Quilt Scene in Miami, Florida, specializing in updated versions of antique quilt patterns. She is a past president of the Ocean Waves Chapter, NQA, where she has been an active member since 1989.

Photo by Juan E. Cabrera

OTHER AQS BOOKS

This is only a small selection of the books available from the American Quilter's Society. AQS books are known worldwide for timely topics, clear writing, beautiful color photos, and accurate illustrations and patterns. The following books are available from your local bookseller, quilt shop, or the public library.

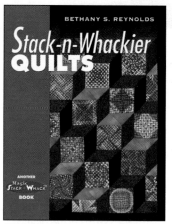

#5850   US $21.95

#5853   US $18.95

#5756   US $19.95

#5755   US $21.95

#5852   US $19.95

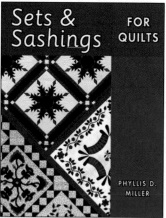

#5590   US $24.95

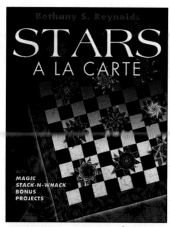

#5589   US $21.95

#4957   US $34.95

#5176   US $24.95

Look for these books nationally or call **1-800-626-5420**